First 1.

# DOG OW .ᴄR

Before and After Complete Guide

## Lee Richards

'First Time Dog Owner – Before and After Complete Guide'

By Lee Richards

Copyright © 2023 by Lee Richards

1st Edition

Limit of Liability/Disclaimer of Warranty

Creative writing can be daunting...

**Misha Herwin**

... a true 'Room in the Roof' writing mentor. Your feedback and support during my creative writing years didn't go to waste and I cannot thank you enough. Your own writing and published children's books are fantastic reads which I and my daughters have loved. A true story teller and fantastic friend x

A true Key Person of Influence...

**Oliver Rayner**

... your help, guidance and mentoring on my own KPI journey has been greatly appreciated. This book coming into being is down to your pointing me towards a future which I hadn't even considered. Thank you for opening my eyes to that which has been right in front of me for so long.

With you by my side I can see clearly, even in the dark...

**Melissa**

...my perfect flame 11:11 xx

I would also like to thank...

Daphne, Ketty, Mark (bro), Paul, Sylvia & Ron, Lee (Tay), Brenda (mom), Shiela and Mike, Rich, Mart, Rob, Rachel, Gill, Donna, Ingrid and
Karima, friend, biz partner and best Dog Behaviourist I know

# CONTENTS

## ARE YOU READY FOR A DOG?

## PUPPIES

# HEALTH AND WELLBEING

# BEHAVIOUR

# DOG TRAINING

# FUN AND PLAY

# FREE BONUS MATERIAL

# ABOUT THE AUTHOR

Lee Richards is a bespoke dog trainer, including behavioural support, based in the UK and Tenerife. He has won several awards year after year in his region since 2018 in dog training and rehabilitating dogs with anxiety, human, object and dog fears as well as phobias and other unwanted behaviours, along with his business partner.

In 2023 Lee became an official Ambassador of two dog food brands which aid dog's health and wellbeing. These are Butternut Box (which Lee can get you discount on – see further in the book) and OMNI Vegan dog food, which has major benefits for your dog's health, body and mind.

As well as being an Ambassador, Lee and his business partner are official sponsors of the charity Yellow Dog UK, which promotes giving dog's space, when they need it most. (See the section on this charity)

Through the years Lee has trained young and older dogs alike and helped many through rehabilitation. In many cases he has created, adapted and evolved techniques to suit the particular dog and family in need. Lee has a large selection of techniques he has created himself to get the needed result/s for a particular family, dog, accommodation and its surrounding stimuli. No dog and situation is ever the same, thus why one technique does not suit all dogs and owners.

In the UK Lee is a bespoke trainer and behavioural support to a qualified and highly experienced Dog Behaviourist who holds a degree in Animal Management, Behaviour and Welfare. He also trains rescue dogs and dogs adopted from overseas shelters, with great success.

When it comes to helping owners of dogs whom have been adopted from overseas Lee enjoys the unique challenges that some of these street dogs bring. Lee is good at achieving the results needed using only positive reinforcement.

Lee's interest in dogs stems all the way back to when he was a young child, and was present at a friend's house, who had two German

Shepherds. As an excited kid, and without understanding that one of the dogs was nervous, Lee leapt up from his seat and, as a result, he was bitten.

There were tears and some confusion as to why the friendly dog would do this, and this is where Lee's interest in dog behaviour began.

Through the years growing up Lee would observe dog behaviour. In one instance at another family friend's house, while young, he engaged in facial expression, body movement and language with a smaller dog. Lee was fascinated to see mirroring behaviour and how the dog was then following him and listening to commands. The dog was intrigued and liked the interaction.

Through his teens Lee got to observe and learn from his friend's elderly dog, Ben. Ben had low tolerance as he was quite old and suffered with joint pains. Whenever Lee got close to Ben, he would give a vocal warning. A lot was learnt from being around Ben.

During Lee's college years he would often, when the weather was good, go into the local park for his lunch. On one occasion Lee got to see a couple training their puppy. Let's just say Lee was late returning back to the college, as watching the training was more appealing than listening to a tutor talk about Art history.

During Lee's early thirties he helped friends train their dogs and considered a future as a professional dog trainer. Lee then met Karima, who is a qualified behaviourist. It wasn't long after that that they setup a successful training and behaviour support business in the UK.

Since then that particular business has gone on to be recognised as one of the best in the local city and county, gaining "best of three" excellence awards as well as other recognitions.

Through the seven plus years working with Karima, Lee gained a wealth of knowledge and greater understanding of dog behaviour.

The next steps for Lee are to create several dog training academies, write a few more books, and help as many people and dogs as possible by doing what he does best.

# So you are thinking about getting a dog?

How exciting!

There are a few things you should take into account before making the decision to become a dog owner though.

Dogs are great companions and can bring a lot of joy to your life, but they also come with a lot of responsibility, cost and commitment.

Caring for a canine companion is long-term, as some dogs can live for 12 years or more. You will need to provide food, shelter, exercise, and medical care throughout your dog's lifetime, as well as giving many hours of love, affection and attention. Plus you will need to get your canine friend professionally trained.

Preparation is key!

Before you buy a puppy or adopt, make sure you are prepared to handle the responsibility of dog ownership.

Research the different breeds to find the one that will fit well into your lifestyle, and be sure you have the time and resources to care for your new furry friend.

This book should help you on this magical journey of discovery.

One dog barks at something...


...The rest bark at him

# Do Your Dog Research

Photo by Jane Almon

There are a lot of things to consider when choosing the right type of dog for your family. Breed, size, and sex are all important factors, but remember that every dog is unique. The way a puppy behaves and fits into your family will depend on how they are treated and trained, as well as their character and temperament. No dog is ever the same. Many breeds do however, tend to have similar characteristics, traits and behaviours.

By doing your research before choosing a dog you can be more prepared, and also give your new family member exactly what is needed for a good healthy life. Below is just some of the considerations when choosing the best dog to suit you and your family.

## Breed

Choosing the right breed is an important first step. Some breeds are better suited for families with small children, while others do better in homes with no children. Some breeds need a lot of exercise, while others are content to lounge around the house all day. Consider your lifestyle and what type of dog will fit best into it.

If you are elderly, frail or not able to move around well, then going with a Labrador or similar breed may not be the best choice as they need lots of exercise, get easily excited and are strong, bouncy dogs.

## Sex

The next thing to consider is sex. Male and female dogs can behave differently, so it's important to choose the one that will fit best into your family dynamic. Male dogs tend to be more independent, while female dogs are usually more affectionate. Again, there is no right or wrong answer here, it's simply a matter of preference. However there is always an exception to how your dog interacts and behaves.

## Temperament

Some dogs are outgoing and friendly, while others are more reserved and shy. Think about what type of personality you are looking for in a dog and choose accordingly.

## Outside Stimulation

All dogs need enough exercise to keep them fit and healthy on a daily basis. Some are content with a daily street walk, however other dogs need to be let off the lead so they can truly stretch their legs and burn off energy.

If you live in the city is there a place where your dog can be let off lead to run about? Or do you need to travel to reach a place where your dog can exercise? Can you commit to doing this on a daily basis?

## Health Problems

Some breeds are known for problems which may result in regular vet visits and medication for healthcare needs in their early-midlife. It is wise to get insurance cover to help with large vet bills. If your finances are already at a push, then consider avoiding breeds with known medical conditions, as you won't want your beloved four-legged friend to suffer due to lack of money. Pugs are known for breathing problems. Cavalier King Charles Spaniels are known for heart problems. Do your research.

Taking the time now to consider the best dog that will fit well within your household is very important. Get it wrong and you may need to change your lifestyle, where you live and much more to suit your dog.

# Costs of Owning a Dog

Photo by Andrew Pons

Purchasing a Puppy can be expensive, so be prepared for some upfront and ongoing costs. But don't let this put you off, you just need to be fully aware before you commit to owning a dog. Adopting a dog tends to come with other costs from the offset, including medication, training and possibly behavioural support.

## Puppy

Before your pup arrives you will need to purchase a few items, which include a bed, crate, puppy food, toys, collar, lead, puppy pads for toilet training and a KONG to help with dealing with separation anxiety. It is always best to make a list of what you need and want, then factor this into your budget, but always be mindful, you may need to spend on the unexpected.

More long-term costs to factor in include dietary requirements, insurance, vet fees, boarding while away from home, and vaccinations.

## Adopting

Adopting from a rescue centre tends to come with training and behavioural costs which can soon rack up. In addition you may find the insurance for your dog will be much higher than having a puppy. Vet visits may be more frequent along with medication needs as well. For the more elderly recue you may need supplements, special diet as well as hydro therapy visits.

## Rescue From Overseas

I come across many people who have rescued a dog from overseas. Most recently was Ralph from Southern India, Boris from Greece and Dave from Cyprus. It is lovely to see people adopting and bringing over to their home country their new four-legged family member. It isn't cheap either.

Consider the following:

- Vaccinations

- Quarantine costs (kennel)

- Flights

- Doggie Passport

- Specialised training for street dogs (I offer this)

- Behavioural support (possibly from qualified Behaviourist)

- Special diet

# Space for a Growing Dog

Photo by Jamie Street

Dogs need a lot of space to move around, so your home needs to be just right for the breed and size of dog you want to own.

## Home

Make sure to have enough room for toys, food and for your four legged friend to stretch and exercise, as well as a place to relax when tired. Big dogs can get stressed in small confined spaces and tend to need more exercise.

Sometimes your beloved canine companion can feel overwhelmed or stressed, so it is always good for your dog to have a place to retreat to. This could be a mat, bed or a crate partly covered by a blanket or beach towel. Having a safe space is really important for the well-being, mental and emotional health of your dog.

## Exercise

Consider your location. Is there a dog friendly park/field nearby where your dog can run off lead and be able to have positive interactions with other dogs and people?

Ongoing socialisation from an early age is vital for good behaviour in your dog. This can also help in reducing uncertainties, fears and anxieties of interactions with others.

Getting this right can save you a lot of time and money. Get it wrong and you may need the help of a qualified dog behaviourist, which does not come cheap. Plus you don't want your dog to suffer as a result of negative interactions, lack of exercise and socialisation.

## Travel

Getting from one location to another can be a challenge when owning a dog. Firstly is the vehicle you intend to use suitable for the size of dog you intend to have? You don't want your dog to not have enough room to move about, adjust and get comfortable whether on short or long journeys.

Consider how you will keep your canine companion safe while on the move. There are several options available including seatbelt click-in's, harnesses, a crate, dog-safe hammocks and much more. Do your research and make sure to read the reviews, especially the 1 and 2 star reviews, as these can sometimes make you aware of possible problems you will want to avoid.

# Choosing the Right Breed

Photo by Wade Austin Ellis

# Gundogs

Gundogs were originally bred and trained to find, point and retrieve game birds. This includes waterfowl such as ducks and geese. Gundogs include breeds such as setters, pointers, retrievers and spaniels.

Of these, the Labrador Retriever is by far the most popular pet dog. They are intelligent, good natured and easy to train. Labs make great family pets and are excellent with children. They are also ideal as support and care dogs for the blind.

If you're thinking of getting a gundog, be sure to do your research first. Some breeds require more exercise than others and some may not be suitable if you have other pets in the house. But if you choose the right breed for you, you'll have a loyal and loving companion for many years to come.

Gundogs can be intense and certainly need a lot of stimulation, walks in the wilderness as well as activities to keep them focused. For indoors consider getting a Snuffle Mat and other engaging games. Make sure to get out into the countryside as often as possible.

# Hounds

Hounds were originally used for hunting, either by sight or by scent. Today many hounds are kept successfully as pets and can live with other animals.

Sight hounds include the Afghan Hound, Borzoi, Greyhound and Saluki. These dogs are known for their high prey drive and their keen ability to spot small moving targets from a great distance.

Scent hounds include the Beagle and Bloodhound. These dogs have an exceptional sense of smell and can track game over long distances. They are often used in law enforcement to find missing persons or illegal substances.

If you are considering adding a hound to your family, be sure to do your research to find the right breed for your lifestyle, home and surrounding environment. Hounds are wonderful companions and can bring a lot of joy to your life.

Exercise is a must. At least 1 hour minimum per walk (adult dog) else expect unwanted behaviour and mischief. Professional training is definitely needed with these breeds, especially with Beagle's who need good recall and obedience.

# Pastoral Dogs

Pastoral dogs have been bred for centuries to herd cattle, sheep, and other animals. These dogs come in a variety of sizes, from the Collie family to the Finnish Lapphund, and are known for their loyalty and hard work. Pastoral dogs are an essential part of any farm or ranch, and their skills are still very much in demand today. If you're looking for a hardworking and loyal companion, consider adding a pastoral dog to your family.

They are not recommended for people living in the city. Pastoral dogs thrive in the countryside. Lots of daily exercise is a must.

# Pure-bred and Cross-breed

When you're looking for a new dog, you have to decide whether you want a pure-bred or cross-breed. There are advantages and disadvantages to both, so it's important to do your research before making a decision.

If you choose a pure-bred dog, you'll know exactly what to expect in terms of appearance and temperament. This can be helpful if you're looking for a dog that will fit into a specific role in your life (e.g., working dogs). However, pure-bred dogs are often more expensive than cross-breeds, and they may be more prone to genetic health problems.

Cross-breed dogs can be cheaper and healthier than pure-breds, but it can be harder to predict their adult appearance and temperament. If you're looking for a specific type of dog, it's probably best to go with a pure-bred. However, if you're open to any type of dog, a cross-breed might be the way to go.

## Toy Dogs

Toy dogs are popular pets for many reasons. They are often small and easily transportable, making them ideal for people who live in apartments or other small spaces. They also tend to be relatively low-maintenance compared to larger breeds, and can be content with minimal exercise.

Many toy dog breeds were originally bred as companion or lap dogs, and they still excel in this role today. Some of the most well-known toy breeds include the Chihuahua, Maltese, Paillon, Pekingese, Pomeranian, Pug and Yorkshire Terrier.

Despite their small size, toy dogs still require some exercise and training to stay healthy and happy. Without regular activity, they may become bored or destructive. It's important to find an exercise routine that works for both you and your toy dog, whether it's a daily walk around the block or a game of fetch in the park.

If you're looking for a loving and low-maintenance companion, a toy dog may be the perfect pet for you. Toy dogs can make perfect companions for elderly and less mobile people.

## Utility Dogs

Utility dogs are those breeds that are not included in the sporting or working categories, but were once bred for a particular role, although as with dogs from other groups, many are now successfully kept as pets. Members of this group include the Akita, Dalmatian, Keeshond, Poodle and Schnauzer.

These breeds were originally bred for a variety of purposes such as hunting, herding, guarding and even ratting. However, they are now mostly kept as companion animals. Even though they no longer perform the roles they were originally bred for, they still retain many of the traits that made them successful in those jobs. For example, utility dogs tend to be intelligent, trainable and versatile.

If you are looking for a dog that is not too large or small, and that has a bit of everything (intelligence, train-ability, versatility), then a utility breed might be the right choice for you.

## Working Dogs

Working dogs were originally bred to perform a variety of tasks, including guarding and search and rescue. However, many working dogs are now kept primarily as family pets, including Boxers, Bullmastiff, Rottweiler's.

There are a number of different types of working dogs, including polar breeds, such as the Alaskan Malamute, Samoyed and Siberian Husky; and search and rescue breeds, such as the St Bernard and Newfoundland.

Working dogs are typically intelligent and trainable, making them ideal candidates for a variety of jobs. However, it is important to remember that they still require plenty of exercise and mental stimulation to stay happy and healthy. I would highly suggest purchasing a Snuffle Mat.

For a further breakdown of breeds visit **dogsevolution.com**.

# Buying a Puppy

Photo by Mia Anderson

When you are looking to buy a puppy, it is important to do your research. This includes looking into the background of the breeder, and making sure that they have screened the puppies' parents for any inherited diseases or neurological problems.

You should also see how the puppies and mother are kept, to ensure that they are in a healthy and clean environment.

## Do not buy from a puppy farm

*These dogs are kept in awful conditions and are solely used for persistent breeding for money, causing the mother dog to be in persistent poor health, pain and discomfort.* These puppies also don't get the care, love and socialisation they need either. And they can be separated from their mother far too soon.

Neurological problems can be common with puppies bred in this manner.

Make sure to ask the breeder for documentation and information on the following:

- Information about the puppy's parents, and any health issues

- which vaccinations will be given

- worming and microchip information

- what type of diet have they been giving to the pup

Also be sure to ask about the puppy's weight and expected adult size.

When you first meet a potential puppy, it's important to check for any signs of health problems. Look for things like a dull coat, red eyes, visible ribs, sore patches of skin, diarrhoea around the tail and bottom, coughing, runny eyes and nose, possible fleas or parasites, crouched body posture, limping or problems with limbs, weakness and struggling to stand up.

If you see any of the above signs be aware that the pup may not be well, and might need a lot of medical care - something that can be both expensive and emotionally draining and can sometimes lead to a premature death.

Once you've found a healthy puppy, there are still a few things to consider before making the purchase. First, think about what type of dog would best fit into your lifestyle. If you have a small home, for example, you might want to consider a toy or miniature breed. Second, make sure you're prepared to handle all the responsibilities that come with owning a dog - feeding, walking, exercising, grooming, and training. Finally, be sure to ask the breeder or shelter staff plenty of questions about the puppy's background and health history. With a little bit of research and preparation, you'll be ready to choose the perfect furry friend for your family!

# Adopting a Dog

Photo by Mohan Vamsi Somireddi

Adopting a rescue dog is an incredibly rewarding, life-changing experience that leads to unconditional love between dog and owner.

However, it is important to remember that when you adopt a rescue, there may have been an unsettled past, which can lead to behavioural issues, if not already present.

## Ask the Right Questions

Before committing to adoption, be sure to ask the right questions from the adoption/rescue centre, and assess what kind of behaviours you might need to work on with your new dog. Will training resolve the unwanted behaviour, or will your canine companion need the help of a qualified Behaviourist, which can be expensive for consultation and training support.

Take the following into consideration before proceeding:

- Is the dog okay around babies, infants, children and teens?
- How is the dog around traffic?
- Can the dog travel well in the car without panicking or being reactive?
- If you have a cat, will the rescue be okay or reactive?
- Is the rescue obedience and toilet trained?
- If left alone is the dog destructive?
- Does the rescue need to be on a special diet?
- Is the rescue on any long term medication or needing regular vet visits?
- Does the dog have fears of certain men and women?
- Does the rescue dog have anxiety/fears with objects, vehicles and sounds?

Be aware of the possible costs associated with dog adoption, from vet bills to food expenses and other financial commitments. Budget appropriately, so you are not caught off guard with extra unexpected costs.

# Before You Commit

It is a good idea to spend some time with a rescue dog at the shelter, take part in a couple of meet and greets, or take them out for a few walks. This will help you to get to know the dog, its character and behaviours before you commit to taking him/her home. The last thing that should happen is for the dog to be returned to the shelter because he/she is not a good fit for your home.

# You Have Just Adopted

Once you find the right dog for you, or should I say, once the rescue dog has chosen you, then the life changing journey begins for all of you.

Okay, so you have agreed to home your new friend, paperwork done. It is now time to take him/her to the family home.

Firstly comes the journey. Taking your time in getting your new canine companion into your vehicle is very important. Make sure to factor in enough time. Don't rush the dog!

It can be a very daunting experience and he/she may have already been through quite a lot. Fear and anxiety are likely to be present. Look for the obvious signs:

- Tail tucking under-between the legs

- Going low to the ground

- Avoidance and trying to find a way to escape.

## Time to Settle

Once you get home, give plenty of space and time for your dog to settle.

*Don't worry if your new friend avoids you or is scared*

Take your time, be slow and steady. It should improve once your dog's confidence increases. Anxiety and fears could remain for a while with some members of your household. Be patient. Consider getting in a qualified Behaviourist.

## Learn and Understand

Every rescue dog has different needs, so it's important to be patient and understanding while working on the settling-in process.

Building a trusting relationship is the key to helping a rescue dog adjust, so take the time to get to know each other and build a routine that benefits both of you. Don't rush it. Good luck.

# Companionship

Photo by Victor Grabarczyk

If you're thinking of getting a dog, make sure you have enough time to commit to the care they need. That means daily walks, training, playing and plenty of love and attention.

## *Dogs are social animals and they thrive best when they have a companion*

Puppies in particular need a lot of care, love and attention, as they are at a very vulnerable stage where being intrigued by everything becomes the norm. Destruction, if left alone unsupervised for short and long periods of time, can also take place.

Having small stomachs and bladders increases the chance of accidents happening in the home, even when trained to toilet on a pad or outside.

It's not just puppies who need lots of attention. Grown dogs need the companionship, interaction and exercise as well.

Elderly dogs need even more of your time to look after them, as there are many things which become hard to accomplish. This can be challenging and upsetting for you all. Patience is key.

## *Taking on a dog is a life-long commitment*

Being a parent to a dog is time consuming and will disrupt your lifestyle, so you will need to adapt, but don't bend too much to your dog, as you have a life as well. Find the perfect working balance for everyone.

Don't let this put you off as the rewards of owning a dog greatly outweigh the negatives and partial disruptions. But you need to be honest and fair before you commit. Can you really give enough time for the dog all through the years?

# Microchipping

Photo by Anna Dudkova

Microchipping a dog is a straightforward, safe and effective way to identify the connection between canine and owner.

It is recommended that all pet owners have their canine companion micro chipped at a young age.

Should your dog get lost or stolen, then the microchip can help reunite you back together.

## Your Dog's Data

The process of microchipping involves injecting a tiny chip, no bigger than a grain of rice, underneath the skin between the animal's shoulder blades.

The information contained on the microchip is then used to identify the pet and its owner if they become separated.

Vets are able to use handheld scanners to read the chips and access contact details for the dog's registered keeper.

It is important to note that while a microchip can help reunite owners with their dog, it cannot be used to track whereabouts or movements. However, if a lost or stolen dog is brought into an animal sanctuary, veterinary practice or rescue centre, the chip can be scanned and the owner contacted directly.

## Pain Free

Microchipping is a quick and painless process, and once done, the chip will last for the lifetime of your dog.

It is recommended that all dog owners keep their contact details up to date on any microchip databases so that reunification with their beloved four-legged friend can be achieved as soon as possible should they become separated.

# Dog Insurance

Photo by Edson Torres

Having pet cover insurance for your dog is essential in protecting yourself against unexpected vet bills.

With a great number of illnesses and conditions that affect dogs throughout their life, it's important to consider the costs associated with ensuring your canine companion receives the necessary medical care.

Medical treatment for dogs can be expensive, and having pet insurance means you don't have to sacrifice other areas of your financial plan in order to cover the cost. There may however be an excess you will need to pay, depending on the plan you have.

Dog insurance also covers more than just medical costs.

If your beloved four-legged friend is lost or stolen, pet cover insurance can provide reimbursement for any associated costs such as advertising and reward money.

Many policies also include third party liability coverage, which means you're protected if your dog causes injury or damages to another person or property.

## A Wise Investment

By investing in pet cover insurance, you can ensure your dog is fully protected and feel secure in the knowledge that you have financial coverage should an unexpected illness or accident occur.

Investing in pet cover insurance for your dog can prove invaluable. The majority of my clients over the years have had pet cover. However I have had a few clients who have chosen to place the insurance monthly payment into an ISA instead. Which is the best solution is hard to say. However just keep in mind you never know what is around the corner.

# Always shop around for the best quote & cover

Taking time getting the right policy can make sure you are covered for all you need, especially if the dog breed you have is known for health issues further down the line.

Also, go through the terms and conditions to make sure everything is right, and that the cover will be there for you should it be needed.

# Going On Holiday

Photo by Elisa Kennemer

Going on holiday with your four-legged friend can be a rewarding and enjoyable experience for the whole family.

It is important to plan ahead and take into account all of the details that will make your dog's trip as comfortable, stress-free and enjoyable as possible.

## Planning

Make sure to plan ahead not just for your own items, but also for everything you will need for your canine companion. Below is a list of some items you may need to include:

- Food and water bowls
- Dog towels
- Dog bed
- Dog toys
- Dog food
- Poop bags
- Lead, harness, collar and contact details on tag
- Dog mat
- Medication
- Teething items for puppy
- Thunder Shirt/Jacket if anxious
- Adaptil Collar, and plugin if anxious
- Adaptil Spray for the car journey if unable to settle
- Dog Coat if cold weather
- Blankets

# The Journey

When travelling by car, make sure you plan regular stops along the way to give your dog a toilet break and the opportunity to stretch his/her legs.

Consider where your dog will be in the vehicle. Will your dog be on the backseat, or in a crate? The importance is to make sure your dog has plenty of space to adjust and get comfy.

If your dog struggles with travel sickness you will need to speak to your vet. You may also consider making the dog's rest area as comfy as possible, using Adaptil spray in the car to calm your dog, and also try to get your dog to lay down and sleep through part/all the journey.

Should your dog be reactive to people, vehicles, or other dogs passing by while stationary at a junction, then consider putting up a cover on the window where the dog is. This will block off the view and discourage your dog from reacting.

# No Dogs Allowed

If you're unable to bring your dog on holiday with you, then it's important to make sure he/she is looked after in the best possible way.

Choosing a reputable kennel or dog boarder can ease the stress of leaving your pet behind and ensure they are safe, secure and well-looked after.

Ask friends or family for recommendations. If still no joy and you are unsure where to turn, try asking your local vet if they can recommend anyone.

If doing research on-line, check that the carer's are registered with the local council and that they have got certifications and insurance. Also look at the five-star reviews, as well as going through the 1, 2 and 3-star reviews.

## Boarding

If you decide to board your dog, it's important to ask lots of questions and arrange a visit beforehand if possible.

Take a look at the facilities and ensure there are enough staff to take care of all the needs in terms of exercise, food and grooming. Make sure that there is plenty of space for your four-legged friend, and if staying in someone's house, ask how many dogs they have themselves, or if any other dogs will be staying over. Your dog should have his/her own room within the house – all the dogs should.

Remember that holidays are a time to relax and enjoy yourself, so make sure you take the necessary steps to ensure your dog is happy and safe.

With careful planning and preparation, a family holiday, with or without your furry friend, can be an enjoyable experience for all.

# Dog Daycare

Photo by Alvan Nee

When searching for a dog daycare, it is crucial to consider a few key factors to ensure that your beloved canine companion receives the utmost care and attention during their stay at the centre. You want your dog to be safe, happy, and not gaining unwanted behaviours, anxiety and/or fears.

## Safety and Regulation

It is important to confirm if the daycare is licensed and regulated by local authorities.

This ensures that the facility adheres to the necessary safety and health standards for dogs.

## Staff-to-dog Ratio

It is essential to ensure that the daycare has an adequate number of trained professionals who genuinely care for all the dogs in their care.

Having an ample number of skilled staff ensures that your dog gets the requisite individual attention and care it needs.

## Exercise

The availability of facilities such as fields to exercise and play, or regular walks, is another important aspect of a good dog daycare.

These facilities provide your dog with the necessary physical and mental stimulation, which is crucial for maintaining their overall health and wellbeing.

## Reactivity

Reactive dogs, who may be prone to aggressive behaviour, need to be separated from other dogs to ensure the safety of all the dogs present.

Professional daycare centres with experienced staff know how to recognize reactive dogs and handle them efficiently.

## Experienced Team

Ensure that the staff members in charge of looking after your dog have the necessary training, experience, and qualifications to handle different kinds of dogs and situations effectively.

## Don't Hesitate to Move

Getting in with the right dog daycare centre will enable you to have peace of mind and confidence that your furry friend is receiving the best possible care and attention. If you feel that something is wrong and your beloved dog is not happy, or coming home with unwanted behaviours, then consider finding an alternative dog daycare centre.

# Puppies Environment

Photo by David Clarke

When you are considering a suitable place for your puppy to relax, play and sleep within your home, there are a few things you need to take into account.

Firstly, the space needs to be big enough for your dog to move around freely, along with a comfortable area to rest and sleep.

Secondly, it should be safe and free from any hazards which could cause injury or damage.

Finally, make sure that the area is well ventilated and has access to natural light.

If you are not sure whether a particular space is suitable for your puppy, it's always best to be cautious and possibly choose another location within your home. Remember, your puppy's safety is always paramount.

## Growing Pup Needs

Once you have found the perfect place, make sure that your puppy has plenty of rest, as your growing dog is going to need all the energy to become fit, healthy and bouncy.

## Beds

When looking for the perfect bed for your puppy, always look for one that is big enough to allow your dog to lie comfortably in natural positions, as well as stretch out.

The bed should be soft and padded, as well as durable and washable so you can keep it clean. Make sure it is made of safe materials.

# Destructive Pups

Some puppies tend to chew on the corners of their bed which eventually leads to it needing to be replaced. To avoid this and save money try one of my bed training techniques on **dogsevolution.com**.

# Dog Crates

Dog crates provide your puppy with a safe and secure place to stay. They can be used as a training aid, but must never be used as a time out area for unwanted behaviours. Make sure your dog has enough room to move about, and consider how big your dog will eventually become, before purchasing.

Crates can also be used to keep puppies secure and comfortable while they are travelling in a vehicle, though you may find a seatbelt harness may work better and take up less space.

While you are in the house with your beloved four-legged friend, consider leaving the crate door open so your pup can take his/herself to bed if they want to.

Here is a list of items to consider leaving inside the crate:

- padded waterproof mat
- comfy bedding
- strip of material from the breeder, which contains mum's scent
- a worn, unwanted t-shirt from the main carer
- soft toys
- Snuggle heartbeat stuffed toy
- Teething toy/s
- KONG – helps with separation anxiety

- Small water bowl with water (if safe to do so – consider spillages, dehydration, central heating in the room, toileting)

## Toys and Stimulation

One of the best ways to keep your puppy happy and fulfilled is to provide plenty of exercise, both indoors and out.

Puppies love to play games and engage in training sessions, so be sure to set aside more than enough time each day for interactive fun.

Socialising your dog with people, other dogs, and different sounds, static and moving objects is also very important. Without this socialisation the world can be taken as a scary, stressful place, which can lead to anxieties and fears.

Finally, make sure there are plenty of toys around the house, especially chew toys for teething puppies. By providing plenty of stimulation, you can help your puppy avoid boredom and mischief.

# I Highly Recommend

Snuffle Mat. Perfect for foraging for treats, engagement and to bond with your dog in a fun session. I play with Sparty using his snuffle mat frequently.

# Puppies First Night Home

Photo by Sergey Semin

Bringing home a new puppy is an exciting time for everyone involved.

On the first night, your pup may be exhausted from the excitement of the day, or feeling overwhelmed by all the new sights and smells.

It is important to make sure your puppy feels safe and secure in his/her new home and surroundings.

## Plenty of Rest

Your adorable young pup will probably want to sleep a lot so don't worry if he/she is quiet or resting.

Puppies usually sleep up to 18 hours per day, so don't be surprised if your pup spends most of the night sleeping in a corner or tucked away in their bed. However, also be ready for some crying, whimpering and barking. It is stressful and strange, and your pup has transitioned from being around mom and the other pups, to then being separated and joining a new family in his/her forever home.

## Comfort

If your pup is feeling anxious, try to provide some comforting cuddles and speak in a soft, reassuring tone.

You may also want to give your pup something to snuggle up with like a toy or blanket at bedtime. Most breeders usually supply you with a piece of material which has mom's scent on it. This will help your pup to settle in.

## Safety

It is important not to let your puppy roam around the house at night as he/she can easily get hurt, trapped and scared.

A crate or playpen is a good way to keep your beloved pup safe and contained until morning.

Just make sure the sleep area is somewhere warm and cosy, preferably near where you'll be sleeping so your pup knows they're not alone. If having your pup in a crate in your bedroom is not practical, then consider on the landing, or find a room which is suitable for everyone.

## Don't Sleep on the Sofa

If at bedtime your puppy is feeling scared, try to ignore any crying and/or barking. It is best not to give in to these demands as this can make your canine companion think that barking and whining will be rewarded with your attention.

## Toilet Time

Don't forget to take your pup outside during the night for a potty break. Start using a command, like 'Pee poo last time' which you associate with going to toilet for the final time of the evening, until the next morning. By using this command consistently your dog will learn the difference between regular toileting outside, and one before sleeping.

With a little patience and understanding, your puppy will soon adjust to the new home.

Dogs do adapt and cope better than most humans.

# I Highly Recommend

Snuggle Puppy. Helps to aid a good night's sleep, with heart beat sound and gentle pulsating. Worked a treat for when my Sparty was a pup.

# Comfort Toys

Photo by Alison Pang

Comfort toys are specially designed to provide dogs with a soothing and calming effect. They are often made of soft and plush materials, and come in a variety of shapes and sizes.

These toys help dogs relax and feel more secure, especially in new or unfamiliar environments.

Comfort toys can stimulate a dog's natural hunting and chewing instincts.

By playing with these toys, dogs release pent-up energy and stress. The physical act of chewing, biting, and fetching also helps them build confidence and develop essential motor skills.

## Great benefits

There are many benefits in comfort toys for your dog. They can help reduce anxiety and stress. This is especially important for dogs who suffer from separation anxiety or fear of loud noises, such as thunderstorms or fireworks.

Comfort toys can also promote better sleep habits and alleviate boredom.

In addition to their therapeutic benefits, comfort toys can also be used as training tools.

Comfort toys are an essential part of your dog's well-being. They provide a source of comfort, entertainment, and security.

# I Highly Recommend

Fluffy soft plush comfort fleece blanket. Sparty absolutely loved his. It lasted him a couple of years before we got him an upgrade for bigger dogs.

# Puppy Socialisation

Photo by Bruce Warrington

One of the most important things you can do for your puppy is to socialise him/her with positive experiences.

Socialisation means exposing your puppy to a variety of people, places, and experiences in a positive way so your pup can learn to cope with new situations.

Too many dogs end up with problems due to lack of socialisation. These problems can include reactivity, anxiety, hyperactivity, excessive barking, aggression, resource guarding, and poor manners. All of these can be attributed, in part, to lack of socialisation.

## Positive Interactions

Make sure your puppy has positive experiences with as many different people, places, and things as possible. The earlier you start socialisation, the better. Puppies should be socialised starting at around 8 weeks of age.

Here are some ideas for ways to socialise your puppy:

- Take on walks in different neighbourhoods so they can see and hear new things.

- Visit friends and family members' homes, especially if they have dogs of their own. Be aware to carefully introduce both dogs outside before entering the other dogs' home. It is best to keep all toys, treats and food out of reach of both dogs – make the experience balanced and neutral as possible. Read one of my articles on **dogevolution.com** for further help and                                                                          guidance)

- Attend puppy socialisation and/or obedience classes. (make sure they don't have any reactive dogs attending, as this could lead to a negative interaction, which could affect your dog's confidence)

- Take them to different types of public places, such as the park, the beach, pet stores, the vets and so on. Try not to overwhelm to begin with, steady steps. So try to avoid overly crowded places straight away.

- Expose your pup to different kinds of people, such as babies, infants, children, teens and seniors.

Remember, socialisation is all about exposing your puppy to new things in a positive way. Never force your dog into a situation that he/she will be uncomfortable with.

Avoid raising your voice when you can see your canine companion is scared, anxious or overwhelmed.

With patience and consistency, you can help your puppy grow into a confident and well-adjusted adult dog.

## Periods of dog development:

Neonatal: birth – 2 weeks

Transitional: 2-3 weeks

Socialisation: 3-12 weeks

Juvenile: 12 weeks to maturity

Adulthood: 1-3 years

What happens or doesn't happen with your puppy has a big impact on the rest of your dog's life in a positive or negative way. Avoidance isn't always the best way. Slow and steady introductions, sometimes at a distance, can save you a lot of headaches, and upset for your beloved four-legged friend.

Socialisation Guidance:

- Socialisation with people needs to be completed by 12 weeks

- Bite inhibition and socialisation with positive dogs by 18 weeks – avoid reactive dogs

- Preventing adolescent problems by 5 months

Socialisation is key to helping your dog feel comfortable around people and other animals, and can be a great way to prevent behavioural issues later on in life. It can also save you a lot of money as Behaviourists aren't cheap.

# Classical Conditioning

There are many different ways to socialize your dog, but one of the most effective is through classical conditioning. This involves exposing your dog to positive stimuli, (with treats, praise, and play) in order to condition and associate those items with good experiences.

Puppies are especially receptive to socialisation during their critical period, which is between 3 and 16 weeks of age. However, it's never too late to start socializing your dog - even adult dogs can benefit from positive experiences.

So, if you're looking for a way to help your dog feel more comfortable around people and other animals, classical conditioning may be the answer. Just remember to start early, be consistent, and have patience - your furry friend will thank you for it!

Classical conditioning is a process of learning that occurs when two different stimuli are paired together. The first stimulus, known as the conditioned stimulus, produces no response from the animal at first. But after it has been paired with the second stimulus, known as the unconditioned stimulus, (several times) your dog will begin to respond to the conditioned stimulus as if it was the unconditioned stimulus.

In other words, classical conditioning is a way of teaching your dog to associate certain things with positive experiences. For example, if you give your dog a treat every time they see another dog, they will eventually learn to associate seeing other dogs with getting a treat (rewarding experience). This can be a great way to help your dog overcome fear of other animals, and can make socialising a much more positive experience.

It is important to note that classical conditioning is a powerful tool, and should be used in moderation.

## Small Paw Steps

If you overload your dog with too many positive experiences all at once, he/she may become overwhelmed and stressed. It is best to slowly introduce new stimuli and pair them with positive experiences, so that your dog has time to adjust.

If you're looking for a way to positively socialise your dog, classical conditioning is a great option. Just remember to start early, be consistent, and go at your dog's pace – he/she will thank you for it!

# Socialisation Checklist

Photo by Emily Star

It is important to get your canine companion used to many different places, sounds, people, vehicles and much more. The below checklist will help your dog to get exposed to many of them. Just make sure your four-legged friend is calm and relaxed.

Make sure to keep the socialisation experiences short, fun and safe to begin with, then increase. Give plenty of praise and treats. Also remember dogs can read your facial expression, body language and tone.

## Hygiene & Health

- Teeth cleaning

- Bathing and towelling down

- Handling paws and using a towel on paws

- Brushing and combing fur

- Clippers

## In The Home

- Stairs, steps and ramps (small dogs)

- Handling by different members of the household

- Washing Machine and Dryer

- Dish washer

- Vacuum cleaner

- Hair dryer

- Noisy and vibrating objects

- Collar, coats, harness and leads

# Out and About

- Short vehicle rides
- Roadsides – vehicle sounds, gusts from passing and heavy clanging vehicles
- Shops
- Vets
- Family and Friends homes and gardens
- Groomers
- Schools
- Parks, bridal paths and fields
- Scooters, Cyclists, skateboarders, etc.
- Shallow water
- Weather - Rain, windy, etc.

# Animals

- Other dogs – small, medium and large, varied colours and breeds
- Livestock
- Horses, ponies and donkeys
- Birds
- Cats, rabbits and other small pets
- Squirrels

# People

- Men and women

- Babies - also in prams, cots, etc.

- Infants – with toys, making noises, moving around

- Teens – with hoodies, large earphones on, etc.

- Loud voices, shouting, laughing, etc. (non-aggressive)

- Clapping hands and making loud bangs (only do when facing and stop if scared)

- Elderly people – with Zimmer frame, walking sticks, wheelchair, scooter, etc.

- Wearing hats, glasses and tinted, face masks, scarves, cycle/motorbike helmets, etc.

- Men with beards

- High Vis jackets

- Long bulky coats, umbrellas, big bags, suitcases, etc.

- Different skin colours

# Puppies First Walk

Photo by Chris Arthur-Collins

Your puppy's first walk is a special experience that should be approached with care and caution.

Before you start your pup on the first steps out and about, on the streets and further afield, make sure all vaccinations have been given by a veterinarian. This will ensure your dog is safe to venture out into the big wide world.

## Preparation is Key

Vaccinations done, it is time to prepare for the first walk.

Start off by making sure that the collar or harness fit comfortably and securely. This will ensure your pup can't slip out if suddenly startled or scared by something loud, scary or highly intimidating.

## Slow and Steady

When you are out on your puppy's first walk, take things slowly. Allow your beloved four-legged friend to become accustomed to the surroundings, without overwhelming them.

Let your pup explore at a pace that suits and take frequent 10-20 second breaks. This will help them become familiar with the sights, smells and sounds of their environment in a safe and calm way.

## Short Walks

Be conscious that long walks need to be avoided for puppies.

Instead, keep your puppy walk short and sweet, to prevent any unnecessary strain on the joints and muscles, which could potentially cause problems immediately or further into the future.

It is best to follow RSPCA guidelines for how long you should walk your puppy, so that you go with the most up to date information.

Preparing your puppy for their first walk is an important part of socialising them. It's a great way to help them adjust to being outside and to make sure they have a positive experience that will last for years to come!

## I Highly Recommend

Halti Leads. I have used Halti leads with Sparty since he was a pup. Now he is 7 and on a large Halti lead.

# Enrichment and Stimulation

Photo by Valentin Balan

There is so much value to enrichment and stimulation for your beloved four-legged friend.

It is a necessity for your dog's physical and mental well-being.

There are numerous types of enrichment and stimulation both inside and outside of your home.

# Inside the Home

You can provide your dog with interactive toys, such as puzzle toys or treat-dispensing toys.

These toys not only keep your dog entertained but also challenge their cognitive abilities.

Playing hide and seek or practicing obedience training in the house can also stimulate your dog's mind and keep him/her mentally fit.

I highly recommend getting a snuffle mat. These have proven results and I use regularly with my clients to increase obedience, a loving bond and so much more.

# Outside

One of the best ways to stimulate your dog outside is to take them on daily walks or runs to new places, not just the same path over and again. Mix it up, even if it is going on different streets. This will make a difference for meeting your dog's stimulation needs and is beneficial for your dog's mental health.

This not only gives the necessary exercise but also allows them to explore and sniff out new scents.

For a big win go visit a new park or go on a hike. Both can offer new challenges and enrichment opportunities.

Another way to stimulate your dog outside is through socialisation.

Organise playdates with other dogs or enrol them in obedience and/or socialisation classes.

This will not only introduce them to new dogs but also people and surroundings, leading to a more confident and well-adjusted dog.

## I Highly Recommend

IQ brain training puzzle games. Sparty has had a few of these IQ games. It is great for bonding and lovely to watch, encourage and see how excited your dog gets.

# Diet

Photo by Ayla Verschueren

To make sure your puppy stays fit and healthy, it's important to feed them a well-balanced diet and give constant access to fresh, clean water. The amount of food portions varies dependent on age, size, activity level and general health. Your puppy's needs will change as he/she grows older.

## Puppies

At first puppy food will be beneficial as it contains the right amount of fat needed for a growing pup. Always read and follow the packaging to give the right amount of food.

## YA Dogs

Young-adult dogs also need to be on a strict diet. Usually this is called junior dog food. It is important to also read and follow the guidelines on the packaging, before moving on to adult dog food.

## Adult Dogs

Most adult dogs should be fed at least once a day and the food will contain the right amount of nutrients and minerals needed to help with joints, organs and digestion, plus much more.

## Elderly Dogs

When dogs get old their diet can become complicated. A lot of the time your dog may suffer from conditions like arthritis. It is always best to seek the advice of a Vet to give your dog the right food to aid in giving relief and much more.

There are a lot of different types of dog food available on the market, so it's important to do some research to find the best option for your pup. You may want to talk to your vet about what type of food is best for your puppy, based on their individual needs, especially if your pup has got particular stomach related conditions.

Also be aware that each puppy food product will be different from the last, so read the packaging and follow as stated, as you don't want your pup to become obese and potentially have liver and kidney problems further down the line.

## Set Meal Time

When you're first starting out, it's a good idea to feed your puppy on a schedule. This will help your dog get into a routine and know when to expect the next meal. It's also important to make sure your dog is getting enough to eat, but not overeating.

It's also important to create a safe and comfortable space for your puppy to eat in. This means having a designated area in your home where they can eat their meals in peace. Puppies can be easily distracted, so it's important to create an environment that is calm and relaxed. This will help your puppy focus on eating and prevent them from getting too excited or overeating.

If you have an adult dog as well, then you will need to separate during puppy feeding, as you don't want your adult dog to wolf down the puppy food, as this will taste great to your dog, but not be healthy, and could result in a vet visit.

## Breeders Diet Plan

When you bring your puppy home for the first time, the breeder should supply you with information on what they have been feeding your puppy so that you can continue with the diet plan. This can either be wet, dry or a mixture of both. If your puppy is the runt of the pack you may also find that they have put them on a separate raw diet to help build their weight up.

Avoid giving your puppy human food, this could lead to unwanted behaviour, begging and also refusal to eat dog food. In addition our food does not always give the dietary ingredients needed for a growing dog. Also be aware that some human foods are dangerous, poisonous and even deadly to dogs. Grapes, seeds, onions, chocolates are just a small number of items not good for your dog. If unsure do your research and stay safe. Avoid human food to be safe, and to give your dog a healthier, better start in life.

# Vegan Diet

Photo by Wannes De Mol

OMNI is a delicious and healthy, planet friendly dog food, which was founded by Veterinarian, Dr. Guy Sandelowsky.

It is made by vets and scientists with the best premium ingredients tailored for dogs of all ages.

Optimised for health and is protein, fat, vitamins and minerals rich.


Extra benefits include (based on a study):

- Coat glossiness

- Less or no dandruff

- Improvements in behaviour

- Less flatulence

- Stool consistency improvements


Excellent for dogs with allergies and sensitive stomachs.

All of the ingredients are blended and steam-baked at regular oven temperatures to maintain their vitality.

By moving on to a vegan diet for your dog we can also help remove more animals from the food chain.

Visit **omni.pet** today

# Health Checks

Photo by Brooke Cagle

When it comes to the health and well-being of your dog, regular health checks are essential.

Performing these checks on a regular basis can help to identify any potential issues early on, which can not only save you money in the long run, but also ensure that your beloved dog is healthy and happy.

## Nose

Most dog's noses are cold and wet. However, some dogs can have warm and dry noses. Whether it is either of these you will need to check for health problems.

You will also want to check for the following:

- Excessive discharge

- Dryness and flaking

- Soreness

If you notice any of these make sure your dog is drinking enough water and eating normally. You may need to take your dog to the vets. Also check for any signs of pain, discomfort or new odd behaviour. If unsure consult your local veterinary practice.

## Teeth

Dental health is crucial for dogs, as it can impact their overall health and well-being.

Look for signs of tartar build-up, redness or swelling of the gums, and any loose or broken teeth.

If you notice any of these signs, it is important to take your dog to a veterinarian for further evaluation and treatment.

# Body and Weight

Examine your dog's body for any lumps, bumps, or unusual growths. These can be a sign of cancer, skin issues, or other health concerns.

Check your dog's weight regularly to ensure that he/she is not gaining or losing too much weight, which can also be a sign of health issues.

# Ears

Checking your dog's ears is another important part of regular health checks.

Look for any signs of redness, swelling, discharge, or odour, as these can indicate an ear infection or other health issues.

Clean your dog's ears regularly to prevent infections from occurring.

# Paws

Look for any signs of cuts or abrasions, and check for any objects stuck in between the pads on your dog's feet.

Be sure to trim your dog's nails regularly to prevent them from becoming too long and causing discomfort or pain.

If you are unsure or find something which doesn't look or feel right, contact your local vet.

# Eyes

Dogs can and do get a certain amount of discharge from the corner of their eyes. Usually black in colour.

As dogs get older you will notice their eyes become smoky. This is a sign of possible cataracts.

Your dog's eyes can give you clues that there may be something wrong which may need the help of a veterinarian. Here are a few things to look for:

- Excessive watering of the eyes.

- Constantly rubbing the eye with the paw, or up against an object or furniture.

- Closing one eye or squinting, which is usually a sign of pain, or something in the eye.

- More red or pink of the skin around the eyes.

- The usual white of the eyes are pink/red in colour.

# Plenty of Rest

Photo by Sarandy Westfall

It is crucial to understand that puppies require a considerable amount of sleep to support their physical and mental development.

Ensure that your dog has adequate time to rest at home.

Similarly, rescue dogs that you adopt may have undergone traumatic experiences, leading to anxiety, confusion, and fear. To help your dog cope with the transition, allowing him/her plenty of rest is critical.

# Sleep

Research has shown that dogs of all breeds require an average of 12-14 hours of sleep per day, with some requiring up to 18 hours.

Puppies, on the other hand, require even more sleep, with some needing up to 20 hours a day.

Sleep is essential for their cognitive development and aids in the growth and regeneration of their body tissues.

# Adopted Dogs

When bringing home a rescue dog, it's vital to be mindful of their sleep patterns and needs. During the first few days or even weeks, the new environment may overwhelm them, causing them to feel anxious, stressed, or fearful.

# Quality of Sleep

Ensure that your new companion has a comfortable space to sleep in and minimize any disturbances, especially during the resting periods.

In addition to providing a cosy bed and minimizing disruptions, there are a few other things you can do to improve your dog's sleep quality.

Establishing a consistent sleep routine, ensuring he/she gets enough exercise, and minimizing exposure to artificial light at night are all essential factors that can contribute to healthy sleep habits.

Be patient and understanding during the transition period and prioritize their sleep needs to ensure they feel safe and secure in their new home.

Health and Wellbeing

# Local Vets

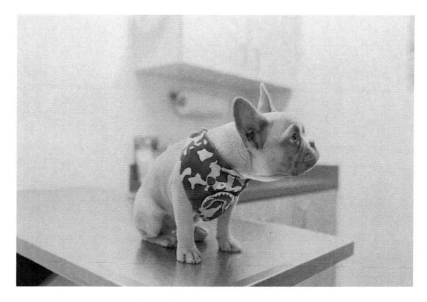

Photo by Karsten Winegeart

Choosing the right local veterinary centre for your dog is of utmost importance. You want a friendly and knowledgeable team that understands your dog's individual needs and provides necessary medical attention which doesn't cost the earth.

# Rewarding Visits

Once you have found the right vets, it is time to introduce your dog for the first time. Speak to the vets about bringing your dog in for a quick hello, where the staff usually give a fuss, a treat and help to ease any worries your dog may have.

Being in a new environment can be stressful for dogs, so it is crucial to create a positive and rewarding experience.

Plan to take your dog in and around the vets several times within the week. Let your dog sniff around outside the vets to get used to the smells. Make it a rewarding experience, so have plenty of treats at hand.

Bring along your dog's favourite toy to help him/her feel more comfortable.

# Reducing Anxiety and Fears

It is important to make visits to the vet a fun and enjoyable experience for your furry friend. This will help in reducing any fear or anxiety your dog may have towards going to the vet in the future.

When you go inside go at your dog's pace. Don't force your dog in, this will make your dog anxious and won't help for future visits.

Once inside be cautious of other dogs, not all will be welcoming and some dogs can be aggressive, especially if not well, or injured. Also don't allow your dog to get too close to pets in carry cases.

# Good Relations

Develop a relationship with the vet and their staff as they can provide you with valuable advice on how to keep your dog healthy and happy.

# Car Safety

Photo by Brina Blum

Travelling with your furry friend can be a great experience for both of you, but it is important to keep everybody safe.

Keeping your dog safe in the car while driving short or long distances requires abiding by road safety and also within the terms of your car insurance policy.

It is important to ensure that all passengers are properly secured before beginning a journey – including pets!

## Dog Safety

Dogs should always be securely restrained whilst travelling in the vehicle by using an approved pet restraint system, such as a harness or crate, or alternatively placed behind a secure barrier where possible. This ensures that everyone remains unharmed if there were sudden stops during travel due to unexpected hazards on roads such as potholes, animals crossing, as well as reducing distractions from moving around freely inside the vehicle, which can lead to driver distraction and thus, increase risks associated with driving errors.

## Insurance Policies

Be aware that with some vehicle insurance policies, if you are in a road accident and your dog is in the vehicle without being securely contained, it could violate the terms of your contract and the insurer may not pay out, which would leave you liable for any costs involved.

In addition to restraining your dog, you should also ensure that they have access to water throughout the journey. Dehydration is caused by inadequate hydration, exposure to high or low temperatures and long periods without food or water. Provide enough drinking water for your pet before starting a journey, and make sure there is easy access to water so they can drink it while on the move.

# Wellbeing and Health

Never leave your dog in the car alone for a length of time as this may put them at risk if they become distressed or overheated.

Keeping your pet safe when travelling should be an important consideration when planning both short, and long distance, journeys with your four-legged friend. Also consider toilet and leg stretching breaks, as well as making sure your dog is comfortable, not cramped into a small space, and can settle.

# Teething

Photo by Tallie Robinson

As a puppy parent, you will go through many milestones with your beloved four-legged friend during their first year of life.

One of these is the teething process!

As the adult teeth start to come in, your pup may experience some discomfort, and this can lead to behavioural issues such as chewing on furniture or other items that might not be appropriate.

It is important to understand that teething is a natural process, and that it may take some time for your puppy to adjust as they go through this transition.

# Step One

The first step in helping your pup get through the teething process is to provide him/her with appropriate chew toys.

These should be items specifically designed for puppies and young dogs, as they are often softer than regular dog toys and may help alleviate some of the discomfort from teething.

I also highly recommend having Coffee Wood, Crinkle fabric chew toys and Milk Bones around the areas where you know your pup may, or has already, chewed. These are highly effective. Through experience working with many of my clients I have identified that surface protection sprays and teething gels aren't highly effective, and in some instances has increased the likelihood of your pup chewing on surfaces, causing damage.

# Step Two

Second, make sure you are providing your pup with plenty of affection and attention. This will not only help keep their mind off of the discomfort from teething but will also create a strong bond between you and your pup that will last for years to come. Distraction works wonders with your young pup.

Additionally, it may be beneficial to give lots of exercise and mental stimulation during this transition. Not only is this great for physical and mental development, but it may also help distract your pup from the discomfort of teething.

## Step Three

Lastly, if your pup is having difficulty with teething, or exhibiting behaviours associated with discomfort such as excessive chewing, you may want to consider consulting with your veterinarian or a professional dog trainer. They will be able to assess the situation and provide advice on how you can best help your pup get through this milestone as smoothly as possible.

No matter what, remember that going through teething is a normal part of life for puppies.

With a little understanding and patience, you can help make the process easier for both you and your pup. With the right care, you can make sure that your puppy has a happy and healthy life!

## I Highly Recommend

Coffee Wood. Hardened wood which doesn't tend to splinter. Sparty used these and so have many of my clients with great results.

# Groomers

Photo by Fernando Nuso

Regular grooming of your dog is essential for good health and well-being.

Prolonged periods without grooming can lead to matting of the fur, tangled fur, and skin infections. Additionally, not brushing or combing your dog's coat will cause a build-up of dirt and debris which in turn can attract parasites such as fleas and ticks.

## First Time Puppy Care

When it comes to grooming your puppy, it is important to wait until they are at least 6 months old before attempting anything more than a basic brush or comb.

Grooming too early can interfere with the natural growth and direction of their fur. This can be damaging for the long term aesthetic and health of your dog's coat.

To ensure the best possible outcome for your pup, it is recommended to engage with a professional dog groomer who is familiar with the breed of dog you have.

A good groomer will be able to advise on the right methods and products that suit your pup's individual needs.

Through regular visits, they will be able to monitor the health of your pup's coat and skin, and provide advice on any issues that may arise, as well as suggesting certain shampoo products to use.

## Experience Matters

At the end of the day, regular grooming is essential for keeping your pup looking and feeling their best. Investing in professional dog groomers can help to ensure that you achieve this goal with minimal fuss. But shop around so that you get your pup into the best groomers. An experienced groomer will know how your breed should look and will also provide a more positive experience for your dog, so he/she will not be afraid to go back.

# Harnesses, Collars and Leads

Photo by Justin Veenema

When it comes to walking your dog, there are several tools that can make the experience safe and enjoyable for both you and your furry friend.

Collars, harnesses and leads are all important items that will provide a secure hold on your pup while also giving comfort.

# Collar

A collar is an essential item for every dog owner. It should fit securely around the neck and should have an identification tag with your contact information in case your dog gets lost. You want to make sure the collar doesn't rub on the neck, causing rashes and soars. You also need to make sure the collar isn't too loose, otherwise your dog may come out of it. This could be dangerous if walking on the pavement of a busy road.

It is best to avoid using a lead on the collar for too long, as this could cause neck problems for your dog as he/she ages.

In some instances, using a collar and lead to train your dog to walk at your side and not pull can be beneficial for fast results. I myself trained my first pup to walk at my side via collar and lead. It took just over 40 minutes to perfect the walk, and after this my best friend walks at my side on and off lead. I do give him a release command to allow him to go ahead, fall behind, if on a trail or path in the park. But I always make sure he has enough time to sniff areas on the walk, which gives me a short break as well. Remember you need to let your dog be a dog, so short breaks on walks is perfect. Once I had perfected the side walk, I then switched to harness and lead.

## Harness

Harnesses provide additional support and comfort to dogs, especially those that are heavier or pull a lot when being walked.

They are designed to distribute the pressure evenly across the chest and shoulders, reducing strain on your pup's neck.

Some harnesses help prevent pulling and lunging, but not all. It is sometimes best to train your dog lead control before selecting preference of harness or collar.

If your dog is anxious, you can purchase a harness which also doubles as a Thunder jacket, which helps with anxiety.

# Lead

A lead is an essential tool for keeping your dog under control while you're out and about.

It is also important for providing an extra layer of safety in the event that your pup decides to wander off. Leads are available in a variety of lengths, thickness, and material so you can find the one that best fits your needs.

Consider having a training lead to begin with. Then move on to a 1.5-2 metre lead. You may also consider using a Flexi lead (retractable).

Whether you choose a collar or harness for walking, it should be comfortable for your pup and provide a secure fit.

When selecting the right collar, harness, and lead, make sure to consider your dog's size and weight as well as their behaviour.

# Worms, Tics and Parasites

Photo by Angel Luciano

It's important to be aware of the potential risks that parasites, tics and worms can pose to your dog.

All three of these pests can have serious health implications if left unchecked.

If you suspect that your dog has any type of parasite, tick or worm infestation, it is important to seek help from a veterinarian right away. Don't delay it.

Your local vet will be able to identify the type of parasite, tick or worm infestation and provide the appropriate treatment for your canine companion.

It is always best to take preventative measures against parasites, tics and worms. One of the best ways to do this is through regular fur and skin checks with your dog, especially if you have been out in nature's green spaces where tics are especially present. Also going for regular vet check-ups is of value.

## The Vets

During health and well-being check-ups, your vet will be able to check for signs of parasites, tics and worms. If they are found, the vet can provide treatment to help get rid of them, and will have the right tools for removing tics as well.

Make sure to do regular flea and tic treatments as well as using de-worming medications as these can help keep your dog safe from these unwanted pests.

## Be Aware

On your regular inspection of your four-legged friend you need to be looking for unusual lumps or bumps on the skin, excessive scratching activity, fur loss, lethargy and changes in appetite. If you see any of these symptoms, be sure to get your dog checked out by a vet right away.

# Dangerous Foods, Plants and Weeds

Photo by Laura Baker

Gardens can be a hazardous place for dogs as there are many plants, weeds and bulbs that can cause them serious harm.

The same goes for certain foods which, if ingested by your dog, may lead to uncomfortable symptoms, even death in the worst cases.

It is important to understand what items you should keep away from your dog and to be aware of the dangers in the kitchen and garden. Below is a small list of items which can be dangerous, and even deadly for your dog. Do further research on foods, plants and more if unsure.

In terms of plants, some of the most dangerous ones for dogs include:

- Lilies
- Bluebells
- Hemlock
- Wisteria
- Rhubarb Leaves
- Cyclamen
- Oleander
- Yew
- Poinsettia
- Tulips
- Dogs Mercury
- Daffodils
- Mistletoe
- Toadstools & Fungi
- Morning Glory

- Hyacinth

- Horse Chestnuts

- Sweet Pea

- Foxglove

- Holly

- Amaryllis Bulbs

- Hydrangea

- Spring Crocuses

- Azaleas

- Acorns

- Nightshade

- Umbrella Plant

- Lupins

- Delphiniums

- Rhododendrons

- Aconitum

- Asparagus

- Ivy

- Laburnum

- Compost

All parts of these plants are toxic to dogs so it's best to keep them away from your pet.

Weeds, such as cow parsley and buttercup can also cause illness, so it's best to be aware of what is growing in your garden and take steps to remove any potentially hazardous plants.

In terms of food, some of the most dangerous items for dogs are:

- Chocolate (the darker the more toxic)
- Raisins
- Nuts
- Alcohol
- Peaches
- Grapes
- Macadamia nuts
- Nutmeg
- Some sweets
- Blue Cheese
- Avocado
- Some dairy products
- Damsons
- Onions
- Bread Dough
- Caffeine
- Artificial Sweetener
- Garlic
- Apricots
- Citrus

- Chives

- Plumbs

- Coconut and Oil

- Cherries

- Nectarines


These food items should be kept away from your dog as they can cause serious harm when ingested.

It's important to be aware of these dangers in order to keep your pet safe and healthy.

By educating yourself on what plants, weeds and bulbs to avoid, and which foods are potentially toxic for your dog, you can reduce the risk of harm to your pet.

Be sure to keep any items containing these substances out of reach and always supervise your pet when in the kitchen around food and in the garden. In doing so, you'll be taking the necessary steps towards protecting your dog's welfare. Remember puppies, adolescent and adult dogs do get intrigued. Not all dogs will identify the danger and avoid. Better to be aware, safe and on the ball.

# Dogs in Hot Weather

Photo by Martin Blanquer

As the temperature rises, dogs are at risk of suffering from heatstroke, dehydration, and even death.

In hot climates, it is important to take extra precautions to ensure your dog's safety and well-being.

To keep your dog safe in the sun, here are some key steps you can take:

# 1

Avoid exercising your dog during the hottest parts of the day, typically between 10 am and 4 pm.

Instead, take walks early in the morning or later in the evening when the temperature has cooled down.

# 2

Provide plenty of shade for your dog, whether it's under a tree, umbrella, or in a covered area.

Make sure he/she has access to cool water at all times, and consider placing a small paddle pool or sprinkler for them to splash around in.

# 3

Never leave your dog alone in a car, even if it's just for a few minutes.

On a warm day, the temperature inside a car can soar to dangerous levels in a matter of minutes, putting your dog's life at risk.

# 4

Watch for signs of heat stroke, including excessive panting, lethargy, drooling, and vomiting.

If you suspect your dog is suffering from heat stroke, move him/her to a cool area immediately and give access to water. Then seek veterinary care right away.

# 5

Be cautious about walking your dog on hot pavements or asphalt. Dog's paws can burn and blister on hot surfaces, so always check the temperature of the ground with your hand before heading out for a walk.

Also be aware of what NOT to do when it comes to dog safety in the sun.

Never leave your dog outside without access to shade and water, and in direct sunlight.

Avoid strenuous activity during the hottest parts of the day, and be mindful of the temperature of any surfaces your dog comes into contact with.

A little bit of extra care goes a long way in ensuring your dog's safety and welfare in the sun.

# Transporting Your Dog

Photo by Matthew Fournier

Whether you're going on a short trip to the park or a much longer journey, it is essential to make sure your dog is comfortable and safe in the car.

# Safe and Secure

It is crucial to ensure your dog is safely secured while driving, at all times. This can be achieved through the use of a dog seat belt or a crate. Just make sure your dog can reposition comfortably without hurting him/herself in the event of an accident, or getting tangled up.

There have over the years been many car accidents due in part to an unsecured dog distracting the driver. More serious car accidents have resulted in dogs having broken bones, dying and also causing injury to the passengers as a result of being flung from the place where he/she was sat.

If not going in a secure crate, always use a harness with a seat belt attachment rather than attaching to your dog's collar, as it can cause serious injuries to your dog's neck and throat in the event of a car crash.

# Small Paw Steps

To make your dog more comfortable in the car, start by taking him/her on short trips to places they enjoy, such as the park or a friend's house. This will help your four-legged friend associate car rides with positive experiences and help reduce anxiety. Also reward going in and out of the car with treats.

Gradually increase the length of each trip, so your dog gets used to being in the car for longer periods.

Consider putting your dog's favourite blanket and a comfort toy in the car with him/her.

## Anchoring

You could also anchor treat rewards, comfort and loving attention to some nice music, which you will play in the car on the journey. I did this for my puppy. I got him to relax in the house, while giving treats, stroking slowly and gently and talking in a calming voice, while playing Alicia Keys, Empire State of Mind in the background at a reasonable volume level. I did this a couple of times through the day for a few weeks leading up to our long journey. It worked perfectly.

## Be Prepared

During all journey's, ensure your dog has plenty of water and regular access to it. Dogs can struggle with the temperature in the car, so make sure your dog is getting enough ventilation, toilet stops when needed, exercise and stretches also. Even if you are going on a short journey be prepared for your four-legged friend. You may break down. If this happens don't leave your dog alone in the car, as this can be potentially dangerous for the wellbeing of your dog.

## Long Car Journey's

On longer journey's it is essential to take regular breaks to allow your dog to stretch their legs, use the bathroom, and get some fresh air. Never leave your dog alone in a parked car, as temperatures can quickly rise, causing heatstroke and even death. This has happened far too many times around the world. People just don't realise how quickly this can happen.

## Fun Experience

When traveling, it's essential to pack all the necessary items for your dog, including food, a bowl, medication (if needed), and a first aid kit suitable for dogs. Taking your dog on car rides can be a fun bonding experience for both of you, but it's crucial to prioritize his/her safety and comfort as well as you and the other passengers. Don't take risks, it's not worth it.

# Dogs in Cold Weather

Photo by Noah Buscher

As temperatures plummet during the winter season, it is crucial to take necessary precautions to ensure the safety of your beloved dog.

Dogs that are left outside during cold and freezing weather conditions are at a heightened risk of hypothermia and frostbite.

Therefore, it is crucial to understand what to do and what not to do during such conditions.

## Best Indoors

Make sure to keep your dog indoors during extreme weather conditions.

When it is not possible to keep your dog indoors, make sure that he/she has adequate shelter, such as a dog house that is insulated with blankets or a safe heating lamp.

It is also essential to check on your dog frequently to ensure that he/she is not shivering, as this is a sign of hypothermia.

## Coats and Jackets

Certain breeds and dogs with thin, short coats, such as Greyhounds and Chihuahuas, are more sensitive to cold weather conditions.

These breeds may need a doggy coat or jacket when going outside to keep warm.

At the same time, it is crucial to not overheat the dog by dressing in too many layers, as this can lead to overheating and dehydration.

## Hydration

It is crucial to keep your dog well-hydrated, even during the winter season.

Water bowls can freeze quickly in cold weather, so make sure that your dog has access to fresh drinking water. Maybe consider having some water with you and a compact dog bowl?

It is also a good idea to place the water bowl in a location that is less likely to freeze.

## Safety on Walks

Avoid walking your dog near icy ponds or lakes, where the ice may not be thick enough to support the weight of the dog. Some dogs do venture out once they pick up on a scent.

Don't use salt or chemical ice melters on your property paths and driveway as these can be harmful to your dog if ingested. Instead, opt for pet-friendly ice melters.

Ensuring the safety of your dog during cold and freezing weather conditions requires proper precautions and understanding of what to do and what not to do. By following these guidelines, you can significantly reduce the risk of your beloved four-legged friend from suffering from hypothermia, frostbite, or other cold-related conditions.

# Dog Behaviour

Photo by Claudie-Ann Tremblay-Cantin

Puppies are very playful in nature, and they often enjoy having fun with toys, people and other positive dogs. Part of being a dog is exploring the world around them, which can include running around, sniffing new smells and scratching at the ground, digging and foraging. These puppy behaviours are normal and should be encouraged through regular exercise and opportunities to play inside and outdoors. Also engage your pup in training, as this can help your beloved four-legged friend learn new skills.

Make sure to keep their minds active and their body well-exercised daily.

# Dog Training

To train your dog effectively, you need to be able to understand how they think and learn.

Dogs learn best through positive reinforcement, which means rewarding them for good behaviour. This could include treats, verbal praise or even just some extra attention.

When it comes to obedience training, there are a few key commands that every dog should know. These include 'sit', 'stay' and 'come'. Once your dog has mastered these basic commands, you can start working on more advanced behaviours and even tricks for treats.

# Positive Thoughts

Mental stimulation is just as important as physical exercise for dogs. Without enough mental stimulation, dogs can become bored and restless, which can lead to destructive behaviours.

There are a number of ways to provide mental stimulation for your dog, including puzzle toys, training games and even simple things like hide and seek. Why not try a Snuffle Mat or a Flirt Pole.

Finally, it's important to remember that dogs need to be taught to listen and obey. This means being consistent with your commands training and making sure that your dog understands what you want him/her to do. It can take some time and patience, but eventually your dog will learn to listen and obey your commands.

With these tips in mind, you're well on your way to having a well-behaved dog that is obedient and mentally stimulated.

# Dog Aggression

Dogs become aggressive for a variety of reasons, including fear, anxiety, feeling threatened, territorialism, warning off perceived threats, and illness. It's important to be able to recognize the warning signs of aggression in your canine companion so that you can take steps to protect yourself, others, and your beloved dog.

Some common signs of aggression include growling, aggressive lunging, baring teeth, snapping or biting, and raised hackles. If you see any of these behaviours in your dog, it's important to remain calm and avoid making any sudden movements that could further escalate the situation. Instead, try to move away slowly and calmly from the perceived threat, while continuing to observe your dog's body language.

If the aggression is severe and you feel like you or someone else is in danger of getting hurt, you may need to call professional help like a Behaviourist. If unsure where to find a qualified Behaviourist, contact your vet and they should be able to assist.

Remember, aggression is often rooted in fear or anxiety, so it's important to try to identify the cause of your dog's aggressive behaviour and address it accordingly. If you are not sure what's causing your dog's aggression, talk to your veterinarian or a professional dog Behaviourist for guidance, support and the right type of training.

With patience and positive reinforcement, you can help your dog overcome their aggression and live a happy life.

# Separation Anxiety

Photo by Matthew Hamilton

Dogs can get anxious when left alone for short or long periods of time. Many dogs associate being left alone as a frightening experience. So it is up to us to teach our dogs that being left alone is a pleasant experience.

There are many things you can do to help your dog feel comfortable and safe when left alone, such as providing them with a toy or bone to chew on, leaving the television or radio on, some fabric with your scent on it, or establishing a set routine for when you leave and return.

*The true effects of Separation Anxiety don't tend to show themselves until at least 25-45 minutes after the person/s have left. The initial behaviour doesn't fully reveal itself. With some dog's they will get emotional and fall asleep, possibly exhausted. Every dog and separation is different!*

With patience and consistency, you can help your dog overcome separation anxiety and make the most of their alone time.

Here are some examples of what you can do to help your dog through separation anxiety:

- If your dog is experiencing separation anxiety, it's important to remain calm and relaxed when you return home. For the first 10-20 minutes, do not give your dog any attention, including eye contact, stroking, patting, talking to, or giving treats. Dogs can read human facial expressions and body language, so remaining calm and relaxed will help towards resolving the issue. If your dog is barking and not resting in the other room, continue to ignore until the designated time is up. (Make sure your pup will be safe and free from harm, and won't damage or destroy anything he/she finds inside

- Ignore your dog for 20 minutes before you leave the house. This means no attention, no petting, no talking, and no eye contact. This will help your dog to relax and feel comfortable while you're away. If you're having trouble with dog separation anxiety, talk to your veterinarian or a behaviourist for more help. Also read one of my many featured articles on resolving with love, Separation Anxiety at **dogsevolution.com**

- Purchase an Adaptil DAP pheromone collar and/or spray.

- When remaining in the house for a long period, the person/s who the dog is attached to should leave the room/house for between 1-10 minutes (make sure to randomise, do not let your dog see a pattern). This will help him/her feel more comfortable and less anxious.

- If your dog is destructive, you may want to consider purposely leaving something in the room for them to destroy. This can provide an outlet for their destructive behaviour, and may help to prevent further damage to your belongings. However, it's important to note that this is not a guaranteed solution, and your dog may still damage other items in the home. Read one of my many informative articles at **dogsevolution.com** for further help, guidance and supportive understanding.

- If you're the one your dog is attached to, it's time to take a step back from their care. Let other members of your household take over feeding, walking and letting out to toilet in the garden. This will help your dog learn to trust and bond with other people, as well as giving you a much-needed break.

If after 1-2 months of following these steps your dog is still showing signs of separation anxiety, then you should contact your vet to discuss other options, such as medication.

# Destructive Activity

Photo by Gabrielle Costa

If you arrive home to find that your dog has been destructive, don't overreact.

Yelling, hitting, or otherwise punishing your dog will only serve to increase his/her anxiety.

Don't raise your voice or scald your dog. Instead, remain calm and understanding.

*Your dog is likely just as upset about the situation as you are*

If your dog is prone to destructive behaviour when left alone, there are a few things you can do to help mitigate the issue.

Firstly, provide your dog with plenty of toys, background noise (radio, television) and chewables, to keep your canine companion occupied.

Secondly, make sure your pup has a comfortable place to sleep where he/she feels safe and secure.

Finally, consider crate training as an option. Crate training can provide your dog with a sense of security, and can help to prevent them from engaging in destructive behaviour when left alone.

## Support and Assistance

A lot of destructive behaviour is done when the main carer is away – Separation Anxiety.

If you notice that your dog is starting to become anxious or stressed when you leave them alone, consult with a veterinarian or certified and/or qualified animal Behaviourist. The Behaviourist will be able to help you create a plan to address your dog's specific needs and help to lessen the anxiety.

Also read some of my many featured articles on destructive behaviour at **dogsevolution.com**.

# Introduction to Other Pets

Photo by Louis-Philippe Poitras

It is important to introduce your new dog to the other pets in your house in a careful and controlled manner.

Proper introductions can help to prevent territorial issues, hyper excitement which can spook smaller pets, as well as aggressive behaviour.

## Cats

When introducing your dog to a cat, it is essential to keep your dog on a leash and monitor the behaviour closely.

Ensure your cat has a safe space to retreat to if feeling threatened.

Allow your pets to meet at a distance, and totally avoid any forced interaction.

Slowly increase the duration of each interaction, always rewarding positive behaviour with treats and praise.

## Fish

Introducing your dog to fish in a tank requires a different approach.

It is important to keep your dog calm and under control to prevent him/her from accidently banging into the tank, which could cause damage and put your fish in danger. Make sure to supervise all interactions carefully and remove your dog if he/she shows any signs of hyper excitement.

## Hamster, Mice and Rats

When introducing your dog to a small pet, it is crucial to keep them separate initially.

Let your small pet get used to your dog's scent by allowing them to sniff each other from a distance. It is also important for your small pet get used to your dog's bark. Small pets can become easily spooked and a direct bark in close range for the first time could potentially kill them.

Always supervise interactions and keep your dog on a leash and get closer to the cage. Avoid leaving your small pets unsupervised with the dog at any time.

Do not let your dog get too close to the cage. Some dogs have had some nasty injuries from small pets. I remember one of my clients telling me of their dog having to have his tongue stitched up by the vet, due to licking the bars of the rat's cage. The rat bit his tongue and the dog yelped and pulled back crashing the cage to the floor. Not a nice experience for all.

Introducing new pets to your household requires careful planning and attention to detail.

It's not just the small pets that could get hurt, your dog can as well. If unsure, keep them apart.

Don't allow your dog to be close by if overly excited. Completely avoid any close contact especially if your dog is reactive, aggressive, has anxiety or fears.

# Dogs with Babies, Infants & Children

Photo by Luke MacGillivray

It is imperative to exercise extreme caution when introducing your furry friend to babies, infants, and young children.

Even the most well-trained and docile pup may act unpredictably in the presence of loud noises, sudden movements, or unfamiliar faces.

To ensure the safety of both your dog and the child, it is crucial to supervise all interactions between them.

Letting your dog off-lead near a small child or leaving them unsupervised for even a moment could result in serious harm.

## Supervise

When introducing your dog to a baby or infant, it is best to start with short, supervised visits to allow your dog to get used to the new addition.

Make sure your pup is on a leash and use positive reinforcement techniques to reinforce good behaviour.

Additionally, it is important to teach children how to properly interact with dogs.

Children should be taught to approach dogs calmly and avoid loud noises or sudden movements that might startle your dog.

They should also be shown how to pet your dog gently and avoid sensitive parts of the dog's body.

On the other hand, some actions should be avoided at all times.

Never leave a dog and a child unsupervised, as a dog may unintentionally harm a child or small infant.

## Dog Tolerance

Never allow a child to pull on your dog's ears, tail, or fur. Such actions could provoke a normally well-behaved dog to react unexpectedly and cause harm.

Keeping your child and dog safe requires proactive vigilance and a deep understanding of the dog's behaviour and temperament. Remember, a dog that has always been friendly can suddenly become aggressive if they feel threatened or provoked.

# Dog Anxiety

Photo by Lydia Tan

It can be heart-breaking to see your furry friend struggling with anxiety.

Dogs can experience several types of anxiety, including separation anxiety, noise anxiety, and generalized anxiety.

Separation anxiety is common and occurs when a dog becomes anxious or distressed when left alone or when their owner is out of sight.

Noise anxiety is caused by loud or sudden noises, such as thunderstorms or fireworks.

Thankfully, there are several ways to help ease your dog's anxiety.

## Small Paw Steps to Confidence

One of the most effective ways is through behaviour modification training. This involves gradually exposing your dog to the trigger that causes their anxiety and rewarding for calm behaviour.

Another option is to provide a safe and comforting environment, such as a crate or designated safe space.

Additionally, there are remedies that can help soothe your dog's anxiety.

Remember, it is important to be patient and understanding with an anxious dog.

Be sure to show plenty of positive reinforcement and love. With the right care and attention, your furry friend can overcome the anxiety and live a happy, healthy life.

*Thunder Jackets can help with anxiety!*

However, it is always best to seek advice, support and training from a Behaviourist or Behavioural Support trainer.

# Dog Fear

Photo by Anna Kumpan

It is very important to be able to detect when your beloved dog is feeling fearful and anxious.

Some common signs to look out for include panting, trembling, excessive barking, whining, drooling and hiding.

These behaviours may vary from dog to dog, so it is essential to keep an eye out for any changes in his/her regular behaviour.

Dealing with your dog's fears can be challenging, but it is essential to take action to ensure their well-being.

# Identify the Source

One of the first steps to take is to identify the source of your dog's stress. This may include loud noises, unfamiliar settings, or strangers.

Once you determine the cause of your dog's anxiety, you can then work on desensitizing them to the situation by gradually exposing them to it.

For example, a dog that is afraid of thunderstorms may benefit from being exposed to the sound of thunder gradually.

Another way to help your dog cope with fears is to create a safe and secure environment. Providing a cosy space where he/she can retreat to when feeling scared, and ensuring that your dog has plenty of toys and treats to keep him/her occupied, can be helpful.

It is crucial to approach your dog's fears with compassion and care.

Yelling or punishing for the behaviour will only exacerbate the anxiety.

Instead, offer praise and positive reinforcement when your dog exhibits calm behaviour.

# Toilet Training

Photo by Austin Wilcox

It is important to remember that toilet training a puppy is a gradual process. It is rare to achieve results overnight.

Some breeders do begin toilet training at a very early stage, which makes your job as mom and dad a lot easier. However not all breeders do this.

## Learning and Patience

For your pup to fully understand the desired behaviour that you want, it can take some time. Be patient and consistent in your approach and avoid scolding your beloved four-legged friend.

## When Not Using Puppy Pads

For fast, effective results try the following:

- Wait until your pup is in position and begun to relieve themselves in your garden.

- Give 2 seconds of happy encouragement in a clap and squeak with big smiles, but don't overdo it. Going beyond the 2 seconds is likely to stop your dog toileting due to being overly excited.

- Now that you have anchored 2 seconds of praise on to the action you are encouraging, remain silent and break off any eye contact and facing in your dog's direction.

- Once your dog starts to proceed to your back door, face your dog and give lots of excitable praise and at least 3-5 treats to make the action even more rewarding.

- Repeat the process until your dog is doing it all the time. Now start to cut down on the treats and begin to faze them out. Keep praise on-going after treats are no longer given.

Remember that with a small stomach and bladder comes the odd accident.

When toileting takes place inside your house do not react, nor say anything. It is important not to feed the unwanted behaviour.

## Using Puppy Pads or Tray

Try the following:

- Dab a sheet of kitchen paper into your dog's wee. Now press the damp area of the paper on to the artificial grass on the tray, or in the middle of the puppy pad. This will encourage your dog to sniff the area and will recognise the smell.

- When you spot the signs your dog is about to relieve him/herself, (which could be circling to find the right spot to toilet) encourage and guide your dog to the tray or pad. If urgently needed pick up and carry your dog over to the toilet area and place on the pad/tray.

- You will need a bit of patience. Learn from your dog's behaviour and watch for the give-away signs.

- When your dog relieves on the puppy pad/tray, praise with words of encouragement and reward with treats once complete.

- Repeat until this happens frequently, you can now start to phase out the treat rewards.

- If using puppy pads start to move the pad/s in stages over several days closer and closer to the doorway where you want your dog to go outside toileting.

- You are aiming to get the pad out in to the back garden or out on to your balcony if living in an apartment. Make sure to weigh down the pad to stop it blowing away or flipping over.

Don't be tempted to scold him/her if there is an accident indoors. Doing so may confuse your pup and set back their progress.

Reward to reinforce and encourage the desired behaviour you want.

# Alpha and Hierarchy

Photo by Kyle Mackie

As a pack animal, dogs are hard-wired to understand hierarchies.

As the owner of the dog, you must take on the role of Alpha in order to establish yourself as leader and gain your pet's respect and loyalty.

This will help prevent any potential challenging behaviour from arising and ensure that your pup understands that he/she is not in charge of the household.

Many dogs can take on this Alpha role, which can be displayed in challenging behaviour towards visitors, growling at owners, refusing to get down off furniture, etc.

# Be Alpha

It is important that you display confidence and assertiveness in order to be seen as Alpha by your dog.

This should be done without resorting to dominance or aggression, as those are not effective ways to lead. Negative reinforcement causes more problems than good. Focus on being a positive reinforcement Alpha, rather than a mean one.

Focus on providing consistent structure and clear rules for your dog to follow, such as setting daily routines and reinforcing desired behaviours.

It is also important to remember to reward your dog for following these rules, as this will help strengthen the understanding of the leader-follower dynamic.

# Alpha's of the Pack

Make sure all members of the household become positive Alpha's, especially with children. However always put safety first - if unsure seek advice and assistance from a qualified Behavioural Support Trainer.

By assuming the role of Alpha within your household and establishing a clear hierarchy between you and your dog, you will be able to foster respect, loyalty, and understanding between the two of you. This will create a positive relationship between you and your beloved pup that is based on mutual understanding and trust.

## I Am Alpha

Additionally, assuming the Alpha role can help deter any potential challenging behaviour from arising in your pup as they will understand that it is not acceptable to challenge within the pack. Instead, your dog will learn to respect and obey your commands and rules, which will create a more peaceful and harmonious household.

I highly recommend letting your dog know that the furniture belongs to Alpha. If you are happy to allow your dog on furniture, then that is fine. You just need to establish a balance, and let your canine companion understand and respect it belongs to you.

It is also of high value in aiding the understanding of the Alpha role by completing the following Alpha training techniques: Alpha Goes First and Alpha Eats First.

# Training

Photo by Amber Aquart

Puppy training helps your canine companion to understand boundaries and expectations that he/she must adhere to in your home, around people and other dogs/animals and out and about.

*Try to do no more than 30 minutes training per day*

With good obedience training you can reduce unwanted behaviours like biting/mouthing/gnawing, jumping up, barking, begging and stealing, plus much more.

## Reward Don't Punish

Positive reinforcement techniques are generally the most effective in teaching dog's good behaviour, as it reinforces desirable actions rather than punishing undesired ones. These techniques work by rewarding your dog with treats and verbal praise after desired behaviour is exhibited.

The use of positive reinforcement should be your go-to training strategy, as it fosters a trusting relationship between you and your pup while avoiding any negative associations or aggressive behaviours.

Avoid any negative reinforcement training techniques and tools. Tools and devices to avoid include shock and spray collars, just to name a couple. Also avoid raising your voice and verbally telling your dog off. Don't hit your dog, grab by the collar or scruff of the neck. Don't pin down your dog. These can get you quick results, however they can harm and set back the bond between you and your dog. and can also increase anxiety and fears in your dog. In addition your dog could express aggression, increase in unwanted behaviours and result in redirected aggression.

# Winning Results

Your training strategy must be consistent, clear and fair in order to gain the most effective results.

With time, care and patience your training will produce a happy, healthy pup with good obedient behaviour.


# Clicker Training

With clicker training you can mark exactly what behaviour you want your canine companion to do via a click sound, and by showing the clicker from a distance.

At first the clicker and the noise won't mean much to your dog. However, after a few repetitions your best friend will associate the clicker to be rewarding and which comes with a tasty treat.

Clicker training is easy enough to include in your training, for better, more focused results further down the line. Just remember the one second                                                                 rule.

## *1 Second apart: Click - Treat*

Have the clicker in view, (trust me it gives better results quicker after a few repetitions) but at least a metre distance from your dog's head. Dog's ears are very sensitive, so being too close to the click sound could hurt your dog, and also possibly cause anxiety and object fear. With the clicker in place, and the treat between finger and thumb, let the treat touch the lips of your dog and take. Within that second click the clicker. You have now anchored a rewarding experience to the clicker and the sound.

Examples of when to click treat:

# COMMANDS

- Sit

- Stay

- Drop

- Leave

- Give

- Come Away

- Come

- Walk

- Side

- Down

- Up

# Fun Games and Tricks

- Circle

- Dance

- Bark

- Tap Dance

- Rollover

- Play Dead

# GOOD BEHAVIOR

- Not barking where your dog normally would

- Behaving around people, small wild animals and other dogs

- Takes his/herself off to bed

- Sits quietly

I highly recommend using a clicker in your dog's training. However like I say to all my clients - if the technique you are doing is slightly difficult, but achievable, then focus on mastering the technique before introducing the clicker. Once mastered and the clicker is introduced, you will find it easier and you will be able to get the rewarding results with your dog.

# Intelligent Dogs

When it comes to training a puppy or older dog, it is important to make the training experience fun, exciting and not stressful for your dog.

Remember that your dog can read your facial expressions and body language. So if you are uncomfortable, stressed, concerned or on edge, your dog will see this, and it can also make your dog's behaviour change. Try to remain calm, enjoy the training experience and make sure that you and your dog are happy.

## More Focused

As long as your beloved four-legged friend isn't a grazer and is food focused, then one hour before your dog is ready for his/her meal begin the training. You should find that your dog is more focused and eager to train and learn.

# Recommended Training Guide

Photo by Anna Dudkova

## Sit

To make sure your beloved four-legged friend sits every time and doesn't hesitate or have selected hearing, you need to get your dog to sit regularly on command. Rewarding with treats encourages and associates sitting on command with a positive experience.

## Wait

You should aim to get your dog to sit and wait for up to 60 seconds. Also work on putting some distance between you. This could be going upstairs, in another room, going outside and out of view. When you are on walks also get your dog to sit regularly at curbs, crossroads and traffic light crossings. It would also be advantageous to get your dog to sit and stay in your local park, on the banks of streams and also to let other dogs on lead to pass.

## Leave

It is important to let your dog know boundaries and understand not to take items and food from the floor, whether inside or out.

## Come

This command is the beginning of your dog's recall training. It is best to begin inside the home with no noises, smells, distractions and stimuli. Eventually you will be able to progress this further using one of many techniques, such as a long lead, at least 5 metres in length.

# Follow

There are many instances inside and outside the house where this command can be important and even vital. You want to aim for your dog to follow you inside to begin with (remaining close), then take the training outside. Completely reward driven. Follow is very similar to the come away command.


# Come Away

This is a great command to get your beloved dog away from something and focused on to you for up to 30 seconds, or until the person, vehicle or dog have passed by. Very good for nervous, anxious and excitable dogs.


# Side

Side walking is beneficial for keeping your dog at your side, focused on you and walking in stride with yourself, whether on the pavement, in the park, path next to waterway, etc.


# Up and Down

If allowing your dog on furniture it is important for your dog to understand that it belongs to you (Alpha). They are allowed on the furniture via invitation however, when asked to get off the furniture your dog needs to obey. This can help towards stopping challenging behaviour.


# Drop

It is important to get your dog to drop on command. You could easily get hurt by trying to prise out something from your dog's mouth, especially if your canine companion is unwilling to let go of the item.

## Stop

When walking you may need your dog to stop suddenly and remain in the position they are currently in. This could be because of a vehicle coming out of a driveway, or mist/fog suddenly descending and your dog being off lead and a distance from you.

## Off

There are many instances where getting your dog to come off furniture, or agility equipment, benches or other objects is highly beneficial.

## Retrieve

This is ideal for when you are outside playing with your dog with a Frisbee or ball, and you want your dog to come back to you with the object to continue the play.

## Away

A simple command for getting your dog to put some distance between you and them. Your dog should then turn to face you and sit or lie down and await further instruction.

## Fetch

Engaging with your beloved four-legged friend using a stick, ball or Frisbee outside is rewarding, healthy and a great bonding exercise.

# Fun Training Commands

## Paw

Getting your dog to give his/her paw for a treat is a fun, cute and engaging command. Some say it is just to benefit the owner and doesn't really achieve much for your dog, other than make your dog more entertaining. However any engagement training increases your bond, gives your dog a rewarding task to complete and gives further purpose.

## Rollover

Once you have your dog down to the ground you could train your dog to roll over on to the side. Many dogs can achieve this quite easily. It just takes time, patience and support to achieve the desired results.

## Bang

Using a command word and gesture with your fingers you can get your dog to sit and raise their front paws in the air, followed by your dog falling backwards or to the side, as though shot with a pretend gun.

## Circle

Some dogs can achieve this quite easily, but not all. Only suggest doing this if your dogs breed doesn't have issues with their back legs at a young or older age. The command is simple. You get your dog to raise on to their back legs with their front paws in the air. This is achieved by holding a treat between your finger and thumb and just slightly out of reach of your dog. Then simply circle at your dogs speed wide around your dog while issuing the command 'Circle'.

## Drums

A fun and engaging command game. Your dog needs to be in a puppy bow position and you need to be mirroring your dog's body language, facing them. Now give the command while tapping your hands a second apart on the ground, excitedly. Your dog is likely to mimic you. Praise them and give a treat reward.

## Dance

You will need to be low to the ground facing your dog. Now tap the ground from one side to the other with both hands as if you are playing a large piano. Give the 'Dance' command while doing this and your dog with excitedly mimic your actions.

## Ultimate Dog Trainer

There are many different types of training exercises and techniques to try for a purpose or simply a bit of bonding fun. To achieve the best results you need to remain consistent, patient and consider how your dog is perceiving what it is that you are trying to get him/her to do.

As well as getting your dog to follow commands you will also want to consider getting your dog to learn to walk on a loose lead and also possibly off lead by your side. This is of great value for you and your dog. Your dog is easily able to check-in on you, and at the same time you aren't being pulled around on a terrible walk.

# Training Options

Photo by Jordan Bigelow

When it comes to training your four-legged friend, there is doing it yourself, group dog classes, online courses or private dog training.

## Do It Yourself Home Training

Training your dog yourself is the most affordable solution, if not free. However, it can be a challenge.

Some books don't clearly explain or show good enough examples to aid the training, which can leave you confused. Online videos through YouTube or other social media platforms don't always explain clearly how to do the technique, and could cause undesired behaviour, destruction and anxiety. It can be a minefield.

It is always best to seek the training through an experienced and knowledgeable dog trainer.

## Group Dog Training Classes

Dog classes are a group training environment where dogs learn alongside other dogs and their owners.

The major benefit of dog classes is the socialisation aspect. Dogs get the opportunity to interact with other dogs, which can help in developing good social skills. However, if your dog is reactive, it is best to seek private training from an experienced trainer.

Usually, group training is more affordable than private training sessions. However, it is important to note that dogs can easily get distracted in a group environment, and may not get the individualised attention they need. All the training offered in group classes is one technique suits all, which doesn't suit all dogs unfortunately. Some dogs need a specific technique to get the best results that work and last. Many people find they need extra training support and training further down the line for their dogs.

# Online Dog Training Course

Online training can be beneficial, but not always.

You need to do your research and read through the reviews of the online training course.

The price for these courses tend to be slightly cheaper than group training classes.

The benefit, unlike group training classes. is that you can go through the training sections and techniques as many times as you like, so you don't miss how it is done.

However online training is also a one technique suits all, which won't suit all dogs.

# Private 1 to 1 Dog Training

Private dog training offers one-on-one sessions specifically tailored to your dog's individual needs.

This personalized approach allows for focused training and can be especially beneficial for dogs with specific behaviour issues.

Private training sessions also tend to produce quicker results because the trainer is able to devote their attention to your dog exclusively and identify the best training techniques to use for your dog.

Private dog trainers tend to come to your home and Local Park as this has been proven to produce better training results.

# Toys

Photo by Carissa Weiser

Dog toys are an essential part of keeping your pup happy and entertained.

Not only do they help reduce boredom, but they can also be used to provide educational stimulation, strengthen the bond between you and your pup, and even help relieve anxiety.

Note that if a particular toy overly excites your dog, leading to unwanted behaviours, it is best to discourage the unwanted behaviour and/or destruction. If that fails then remove it altogether, and avoid these types of toys for your four-legged friend.

If your dog is anxious then I suggest getting toys that are proven to successfully reduce anxiety in dogs. Usually these are interactive toys where you also get involved and encourage and reward regularly.

There are a wide variety of interactive dog toys which include tug-of-war ropes, squeaky balls, Frisbee's and much more. I highly recommend good interaction between your dog and the entire family through bonding, play and learning.

For comfort you can get chew toys, as well as comfort objects like cuddly blankets and pillows. Regular playtime with these types of toys can help to relieve worry and stress in even the most anxious pup.


Here is a list of some of the toys you can buy for your pup, with benefits:


## Treat Toys

Treat toys can be great fun for your dog, as long as used for short bursts. You will want to make sure that the toy doesn't crack, crumble or peel, as your dog will be chewing on it a lot. The idea of these toys is that you put treats and/or food mixture inside the toy so that your dog can settle and lick the contents, which will help to calm your dog. Great for nervous, anxious dogs and especially dogs suffering with Separation anxiety. As an alternative you may consider a lick mat, which tend to be made of rubber. Just be careful your dog doesn't chew the material, so supervise at all times.

KONG Classic is a product I use with my dog, and have suggested for many of my clients over the years, as it is strong and shaped well to aid your dog.

The main thing you need to remember is not over cramming food/treats into the Treat toy, as this can lead to frustration and stress, which usually leads to unwanted behaviour and sometimes destruction.

## Durable Chew Toys

These types of toys tend to be strong and hard to destroy. Ideal for dogs with strong jaw bones. These toys can come with coloured string surrounding them, a squeaky inside, ridged which is good for your dog's teeth, and a variety of shapes and colours. Every dog should have at least one of these.

## Tug Toys

Engaging with your dog with a tug toy is fun, engaging and good for your bond. However, these types of toys should only be used in short bursts. If you have a dog who is anxious, slightly aggressive or hyper excitable, then it would be wise to avoid this type of toy. There are other toys available where you and your pup can engage in play together.

## Plush Toys

These are perfect comfort toys. Most of the time they come with a squeaky inside and come in a wide range of shapes, sizes and colours. You can get anything from a Doughnut to a duck and even a bell clanging octopus.

# Squeaky Balls

These toys tend to be sturdy plastic with ridges or pointy pieces sticking up, which helps your dog to grip and helps with the teeth as well.

# Puzzle Toys

These are fantastic toys to interact with your dog with. Your dog has to work out how to get the treats out by completing a puzzle. Highly recommended, stimulating and rewarding. Every pup needs at least one of these.

# Snuffle Balls and Mats

Another great activity for your dog. You place treats between the material and your dog has to work on getting the treats out. Highly recommended under supervision and being close to the ground with your canine companion, encouraging on and giving a good, short fuss when a treat is obtained from the snuffle.

With so many toy options available you can stimulate your canine buddy for hours, as well as growing your bond and educating him/her at the same time.

Learn and understand your dog, and adapt to the right type of toy based on what works, lasts and doesn't encourage unwanted behaviours.

# Treats

Photo by Wannes De Mol

Treats are a great way to reward and motivate your four-legged friend whether through following commands or through completing a wanted behaviour.

Low value treats are where you will begin the reward-based training. When you get stuck, or need more motivation, then you will progress on to high value treats.

With processed treats progressing and developing all the time, there has been an increase in treats which are in-between low and high value. This is fantastic as it now gives you 3 levels to aid in training your canine companion.

## Low value treats

These can be purchased in your local pet store, supermarket or on-line. They come in many shapes, sizes, flavours and smells. Usually they are long, thin strips, chunky shaped pieces or freeze-dried chunks. Even dog food kibble can be used as a low value treat. Low value treats are perfect for reinforcing basic behaviours that don't require a lot of effort, like coming when you call or following commands like sit, stay and leave.

Whenever purchasing packaged dog treats always read the ingredients. You want natural. Be careful of unknown scientific wording - research on-line as to what this ingredient is and avoid if necessary. Also be careful of certain fats and sugars.

## High value treats

These should be reserved for times when you want to really reward your pup for a difficult challenge or gain longer attention.

Think things like completing an agility course, learning a complex new trick, or even just being really good while taking a bath! High value treats are the perfect way to make sure your pup knows the hard work is worth it.

High value treats include cooked meats, cheese, peanut butter smear, sausage, bacon and egg. However be careful as an increasingly high number of dogs are showing signs of IBS.

It is important to remember that treats should always be used in moderation and as part of a healthy diet.

With the right balance between low value and high value treats, you can make sure your pup is rewarded for the hard work and good behaviour!

When training it is best to do this when your dog is hungry. Also keep the pieces small so your dog doesn't get full quickly and lose interest.

# Conclusion

Photo by Roberto Nickson

Being the parent of a dog is one of the best experiences in life. Some of the best friendships are between owner and dog. Man's best friend.

I have heard time and time again from people I have met in training and support of how they prefer dog's to humans.

It is fair to say that we have a fantastic bond with our four-legged friends.

Just remember a dog is for life and a big commitment.

The dog needs you and trust me, in a few years from now, you won't ever know how you managed to get by without a dog. Most dog owners have more than one dog in their lifetime.

Enjoy the loving, loyal bond.

# Thanks for reading!

I really hope you enjoyed reading my first book, and gained value from the information I have given, from many years of experience and knowledge with training and rehabilitating dogs in the United Kingdom and overseas.

I love dogs and even more so working with them and their owners to achieve rewarding results.

So please love your dog, be understanding and patient and gain one of the best loving bonds you can experience in life.

Wishing you and your canine companion all the best.


Lee Richards

Multi-Award Winning Dog Trainer & Behavioural Support

# Butternut Box Dog Food

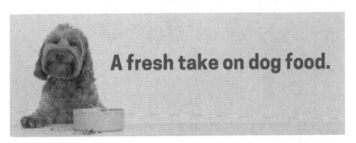

Butternut Box is a fantastic food choice for meat and veg eating dogs. The ingredients are healthy and to human-quality standards. The selection of dog food is really good, and as an Ambassador I am proud to offer you a money saving solution.

Butternut Box is what I feed my own dog, who is 7 at the time of this book going live. Being a Labradoodle he has fur which grows deep inside his ears, so suffers with ear infections and also IBS. Regardless how much we carefully and gently tended to his ears he would struggle. We took him to the vets often and changed his diet over and over again. That was until we were recommended to use Butternut Box by one of my clients who saw improvements in health with their own dog.

Since moving on to Butternut Box, Sparty's health has improved. His IBS isn't as frequent and his ear infections are becoming less as well. So it wasn't long before I contacted them and became an official Butternut Box Ambassador.

Ambassador Special Offer

# 75% off your first box  +  25% off your second

To take advantage of this special offer visit the following link:
www.butternutbox.com/Sparty123

IF YOU LIKE THIS BOOK, HELP ME BY LEAVING A REVIEW ON AMAZON!

1.  Go to **Amazon** and click on '**My Orders**'

2.  Search for **this book** in your purchases and click on details

3.  Scroll down the page and click on '**Write a customer review**'

Your review will help me and others in need of help

Thanks a lot!

**Lee Richards**

# DogsEvolution.com

Dogs Evolution is one of the official websites, where I write articles, give training tips and behaviour advice plus much more, as an official Ambassador and contributor.

As well as myself writing on the platform there is content shared by other dog owners, carers and people in the industry.

Visit **www.dogsevolution.com** today and signup to gain access to features, comments and much more.

Alternatively scan the QR code with your mobile phone and it will take you to the website.

You can also follow Dogs Evolution on Facebook

www.facebook.com/dogsevolutionpage

# Lee's Leave Command

Photo by Alexander Grey

**Note:**  *if your dog bites, fix this firstly before moving onto this training technique.*

For the first stage of this training technique you will need a handful of kibble treats in one hand (clenched fist, behind your back – Rewards). You will also need 3-4 kibble treats in the other hand (held within your fist, with a gap where your dog can smell and stick his/her tongue in).

- Get down to your dog's level, about ¼ metre distance between you both, with your dog sitting.

- Place the treat fist behind your back with one treat ready to be given as a reward between your finger and thumb.

- Present the other fist to your dog's nose (3-4 kibble treats inside).

- Your dog will now sniff and lick for the treat.

- Keep stating 'Leave' (two seconds apart) and also include your dog's name randomly.

**Note:**  *if your dog tries putting a paw on the presented fist, simply keep your fist in the same place and just tip your fist either left or right, and the paw will fall off.  You should only need to do this a few times.  However if it becomes too often with no sign of your dog stopping with the paw, then break out of the training without saying anything and walk away (don't give any of the treats at this time) and leave it for at least five minutes (without giving any attention) then return back to training the Leave command.*

- When your dog pulls away for 1-2 seconds present your dog with a kibble reward from behind your back.  While eating the reward prepare his/her next treat between finger and thumb and place behind your back.

*Note:* *if your dog pulls away from the treat but looks down at the ground below where your fist is – don't give a reward. Your dog is looking to see if anything has dropped from your fist. We are wanting your dog to either look at your face, into your eyes, your chest, stomach, to the sides or at your fist.*

- Do this fist presentation two more times.

*Note:* *if you break out of the technique at any time, or your dog gets distracted, gets up and walks away, you will need to restart from the very beginning.*

- Now that you have presented your fist three times to your dog and three treats been given, you can move onto the second bit of the first stage of technique training.

- Move your fist at least a hands length away from your dog and open it, showing the 3-4 kibble.

- If your dog leans in closer then quickly close your fist and turn your fist upside down (anti-clockwise).

- Your dog should now revert to previous posture.

- Open your fist revealing the kibble. If your dog leans in again, repeat the closing fist and turning upside down.

- You will continue doing this for a few instances until when you have your hand present with kibble on display and your dog does not lean in.

- Once this happens you want to keep your hand stationary and repeat 'Leave' three times (two seconds apart).

- Now reward with kibble from the hand behind your back.

- You will continue this bit of the first stage of training technique two more times.

- Now you will move on to the third bit of the first stage.

- With the kibble on display in your open hand (about a hands length away from your dog's nose) you will slowly start to move your hand closer towards your dog's nose, while repeating three times 'Leave'.

- If your dog leans in, then close the fist and return to the position (hands length) to where you started.

- Your dog should now have returned to previous posture.

- Open your fist and approach again.

**Note:** *you are aiming to get the treat almost touching your dog's nose/lips.*

- Every time your dog leans in, close your fist and repeat the process (hands distance away).

- With three 'leaves' complete and kibble been presented up close, then reward with the kibble treat from behind your back and pull the presentation hand back by one hand's distance ready to go a second and third time.

- Once you have managed three open-hand presentations to your dog's nose/lips without your dog leaning in, (achieved three times in a row) break out of the training and put the remainder of the kibble away (do not give it to your dog, as this will undermine the purpose of the training).

- You will need to do all three bits of stage one every day (if possible twice, spread out through the day) for a week.

*Note: stage two is exactly the same as stage one, except the kibble in the presentation hand will be replaced with something yummy (high level treats).  So you will want either a small chunk of chicken, sausage, beef, ham, pork, bacon, cheese, egg – all depending on your dog's diet/health)*

- Once you have completed stage one perfectly for seven days, you can move on to stage two.

- Have a handful of kibble treats in a fist behind your back, and the piece of yummy food in the fist of your other hand. (presenting hand)

- You are wanting each day (preferably twice a day, spread out) to complete all three bits of stage two, perfectly.  This needs to be done for seven days.

*Note: your dog is likely to reject the kibble reward at first, and maybe for a couple more instances.  He/she wants the yummy food.  Your dog may take it, but allow it to drop from the mouth to the floor.  Or may not take it from your fingers and thumb.  If after presenting and your dog is not taking (after 2-3 seconds) then drop the kibble reward to the ground.  Your dog earned it.  After training and the kibble is still on the ground, then ignore it and walk away.  Your dog is likely to return to it a while later.  Don't pick it up.  Your dog earned it – important!*

*After a few kibble treats presented and rejected, your dog will come to realise that something is better than nothing.*

- Once you have complete stage two, you can move on to stage three.

- Now you are going to put your dog to the test.  Stage three.

- With your dog in another room, place a high level yummy bit of food at least one metre away from you.  Now turn away so that you are not facing the food, but able to see it in the corner of your eye the food and your dog when enters the room.

- Once your dog comes in he/she is going to notice the food on the floor, and is likely to look at you (either standing or sitting).

- If your dog eats the food, then continue practicing stage two for a few more days, then repeat stage three. Continue this until mastered.

- Once stage three is done, you are ready to move to stage four (do this a couple of days later).

- Stage four comes in two bits. You will need someone to help you with the second bit of stage four.

- In the kitchen with your dog present, place something yummy on a spoon, and tip the spoon so that the yummy stuff drops to the floor. (make sure it isn't greasy, oily or anything which could stain your floor, kitchen units or anything else)

- Your dog will notice this and look to you.

- You will now direct your dog out of the kitchen, and give a kibble reward. Then return to clean up the yummy food.

- Now move on to the second bit of stage four.

- For this you will be outside with your dog on short lead. You will need someone to help with this. The helper will be at least 4 metres ahead of you and your dog. All of you walking in the same direction.

- The helper will have a piece of something yummy. He/she will place the food on the path and continue walking.

- As you and your dog approach the food, your dog will notice and likely look at you. Talk to your dog and continue walking past the food for 2-3 metres distance.

- Get your dog to sit, reward with kibble and give a 2-3 second fuss.

- Now your dog should be ready to leave any food on the floor in the house and outside. If any setbacks, go through the stages you feel you need to brush up upon.

Important disclaimer: please note that I usually monitor, observe and assist with this training technique in person. Sometimes the training can be read and perceived different than is meant to be. As such, without being present I cannot guarantee the results. In addition, every dog, individual, and surrounding stimuli can change how the training works. I cannot accept full, or part, liability for you following this training technique. You, as the dog owner, are choosing to follow this technique with your dog. However, I have used this technique with great success with many clients and their dogs.

# Lee's Wait Command

Photo by Reed Shepherd

For this technique you will want five small kibble (low level) treats per session of training. Aim to train twice a day, maybe morning and evening.

*Note: for this technic don't adjust your distance from your dog. Keep it the same. However you can do simple wait with distance training to compliment this technic. For this complimentary 'Wait' training you only need to say wait the once. With distance you can try going further away from your dog, circling around your dog. From circling you can try spiralling. Try going out of sight, up and down stairs, behind doors.*

- Place a kibble treat between finger and thumb, come down to your dog's level, or stand before your dog.

- Get your dog to sit and present the treat (hands distance from your dog's nose)

- Say 'Wait'

- Count in your head to two seconds.

- Repeat 'Wait' – however stretch out the command going slightly louder (this is important as a distractor to your dog's distraction further down the line, plus it will anchor to the final command)

- Count in your head to two seconds.

- Say 'Wait' and present the treat to your dog's lips to take within 1 second of giving the command.

- Repeat this technic until all five treats are eaten.

*Note:* *this training technic will ultimately get your dog to sit and wait for up to 60 seconds.  We are building your dog up to wait patiently and control any excitement and easy distraction issues experienced.*

- You will do the above for three days in a row.

- Once the three days are complete, change your two second gaps to four seconds and continue training for another 3 days.

- You will continue the above (increasing 2 seconds every three days on both gaps) until you reach 60 seconds.

*Note:* *I highly recommend doing Mat training at the same time as building this up.  Mat training is pretty awesome as it works as a safe/happy place for your dog, but also a place for you to issue the command to go to when the doorbell rings, allowing you to answer the door easily without your dog scrambling to get past you to the visitor.*

Important disclaimer: please note that I usually monitor, observe and assist with this training technique in person. Sometimes the training can be read and perceived different than is meant to be.  As such, without being present I cannot guarantee the results.  In addition, every dog, individuals and surrounding stimuli can change how the training works. I cannot accept full, or part, liability for you following this training technique.  You, as the dog owner, are choosing to follow this technique with your dog.  However, I have used this technique with great success with many clients and their dogs.

This training technique is copyright © of Lee Richards 2022, and cannot be used by any other dog trainers, behaviourists, dog training specialists, without the written agreement from Lee Richards.  If interested in using this technic please email Lee directly.  Email is towards the back of the book.

# 1 2 3 Walk

Photo by Edgar Chaparro

Our beloved four-legged friends can and do easily get distracted on walks and want to sniff and engage with many things. This can make getting the much needed exercise a difficult challenge and can also be frustrating for the person walking the dog. In most of these instances the dog doesn't get anywhere near enough exercise, due to sacrificing walk time to sniffing, investigating and doing what dogs generally like to do.

So we don't want the exercise to suffer, nor do we want to stop our dog from sniffing and being a dog. We need a balance. That is where this technique comes in.

**Note:** *for this technique you will need low level dog treats for rewarding.*

## Start of the Walk (1)

- Select a lamppost, car, tree or something else to aim for. (approx. 15 metres from your start position)

- Before you start the walk to the first objective which you have set, give your dog a treat, loosen the lead (if safe to do so) so that your dog can sniff for 30 seconds.

- Once the 30 seconds are done, commence the walk to the set objective location.

- During this walk hold the lead close so that your dog can't quite reach a possible distraction to his/her side. However don't hold the lead too tight that it is straining your dog.

- If you notice your dog trying to go in for a sniff increase your walk speed until you are past the distraction, then slow back down to the normal walk speed.

- Continue being Alpha, controlling the walk.

- As soon as you reach the lamppost, tree, etc. then stop, loosen lead if safe to do so. Give your dog a treat and allow your dog 30 seconds to sniff.

## Walk (2)

- During the 30 second break your dog is having for passing the first objective (lamppost, etc.) set the next objective. This will be double from the first. So approx. 30 metres distance from your current position. Once you see the car, tree, lamppost, etc. that you are to reach without dog sniffing wait for your dog's 30 seconds to complete.

- Commence the walk, not allowing your dog to sniff during the walk (speed up past the distraction – remember not to yank on the lead).

- Once you reach the objective, stop, reward with a treat and allow your dog to sniff for 30 seconds.

## Walk (3)

- While your dog is enjoying the 30 seconds of sniff time, you want to set the next objective. This time is needs to be about 45 metres distance from your current position.

- Once 30 seconds complete continue on with the (no sniffing) walk to the new objective.

- At this objective reward and allow 30 seconds of sniff time.

# And Repeat (3)

- For the rest of the walk you need to keep setting objective waypoints to stop, reward and allow 30 seconds of sniff time. Each of these will be roughly 45 metres from each position you are in.

- Continue this until you reach your home or car to end the walk. Make sure to give a treat and 30 seconds before going inside and ending the walk.

*Note: continue the above until your dog fully gets used to reaching the way points without trying to pull towards something to sniff while in a walk.*

*Once this is achieved now start to increase the distance before your dog gets a treat and 30 second sniff time. You can then choose through training how often your dog is to stop to sniff on a walk.*

**Important:** be aware of signs from your dog when needing to pee or poo. Make sure to stop, then once all done and everything cleaned up, continue on to the set waypoint.

# Mat Training

Photo by John Salzarulo

Mat training is an ideal way to help control your dog when people are at your front door. Once trained the mat can be used for holidays or staying with other family members and friends. The mat is a happy positive place for your dog, and must not be used for time out, punishment, or for long periods of time.

## Stage one (sprinkles)

- Place the mat in an area where you won't walk or trip over it, preferably in a quiet place to train. Make sure that the mat is not on a slippery or shiny surface where the mat can easily move about. In addition make sure that when you put the mat down in the new location that you don't let your dog see you place it on the ground as this could lead to your dog turning the mat into a play object.

Make sure all edges are perfectly down to the ground and nothing is sticking up where your dog could chew, lift, drag away or paw.

- For 1 week (without your dog seeing you do this) scatter 2-3 small treats in the middle of the mat a couple of times per day.

## Stage two (behaviour and interest)

- Be close by to the mat (within 1-2 metre distance). Have treats ready in your hand. If clicker training, have that ready as well.

- Call your dog over (if not already) to sit. Walk slight distance from your dog, not giving any further attention. However be on the lookout for your dog to do one of the following triggers:

- Look at the mat. Sit on the mat. Place one or more paws on the mat. Lie down on the mat. Smell the mat.

- If your dog does any of the above then place a treat on to the mat. (click)

- Don't try to force your dog onto the mat, as the mat is a fun place, and must not be used in a negative manner.

- Wait until your dog goes away from the mat. (if your dog does not leave the mat, throw a small treat a short distance away from the mat, so that your dog will leave to get it)

- Repeat the above technic as often as you see your dog complete one of the triggers, but don't over feed, as this could turn it into a new game which we don't want to happen.

- Stage two is to be done daily for up to 1 week. In addition during this phase keep sprinkling treats on the mat when your dog does not notice and isn't around.

## Stage three (command)

- Let your dog see you place a couple of treats on the mat, and say 'on your mat'.

- Now call your dog off and away from the mat (1-2 metres) with a treat visible between your fingers. Get your dog to sit and wait. Then move over to the mat and place the treat in the middle of the mat and say 'on your mat' and gesture your dog to take the treat.

- Repeat the above 3-5 times daily for up to 2 weeks.

- Continue to sprinkle treats on the mat when your dog is not present.

## Stage four (time on the mat)

- Follow stage three technique, however now get your dog to sit or lie down on the mat and wait. Start with 10 seconds and then reward to the mat.

- You are aiming to increase up to 30 seconds before rewarding your dog. (wait command training will benefit you here and shorten the time to train)

## Stage five (release command)

- Follow stage three technique, however now you are aiming to get your dog to sit or lie down on the mat for up to 1 minute.

- Once the time is up, reward your dog and congratulate, and release him/her from the mat, with a release command, like 'Ok' and gesture your dog from the mat.

- You are now aiming to increase up to 3 minutes before rewarding your dog.

## Stage six (the look and visit)

- Stand 2-3 metres away from the mat. Also make sure your dog is a distance from the mat as well.

- Call your dog's name followed by 'on your mat'.

- If your dog looks at the mat or goes over to the mat reward with a treat to the mat and give a fuss.

- Continue doing this once or twice per day for 2 weeks.

## Stage seven (distractor)

- Continue stage six technique, however now add a distractor. The distractor can be another person making noises, dancing or moving around in a silly manner.

- Continue practicing this until your dog goes to the mat and not to the distractor (every time)

## Stage eight (distractor + sit)

- Continue stage seven technique, however now get your dog to sit for up to 1 minute, then reward treat to the mat and give a fuss

- Work towards Increasing the time sitting on the mat up to 3 minutes.

## Stage nine (one room to the next)

- Continue stage seven technique, however this time yourself and your dog need to be in a different room to the mat.

- Keep moving the mat to different rooms to encourage your dog to find the mat, sit on it until you give the release command, regardless of any distractions going on.

## Stage ten (front door staged)

- Once you have mastered stage nine, you can attempt a real life scenario. (staged – needs an Alpha and a visitor and the mat needs to be moved into entrance area where front door is)

- When you hear the front door knock, or doorbell ring, give your dog the command 'on your mat', and make sure your dog gets on to the mat before opening the door.

- Answer the door. However keep a side view on your dog.

- If your dog leaves the mat, close the door (don't let the visitor in) and sternly (but not aggressively) tell your dog 'on your mat', making eye contact and facing your dog.

- Go to open the front door again and repeat as many times as needed.

- Eventually you will be able to get the visitor through the hallway and into the sitting room, where you can then sit down and release your dog from the mat.

- Now reward.


Remember that the mat can go anywhere, however your dog needs to know where it is to follow the 'on your mat' command.


Important disclaimer: please note that I usually monitor, observe and assist with this training technique in person. Sometimes the training can be read and perceived different than is meant to be. As such, without being present I cannot guarantee the results. In addition, every dog, individuals and surrounding stimuli can change how the training works. I cannot accept full, or part, liability for you following this training technique. You, as the dog owner, are choosing to follow this technique with your dog. However, I have used this technique with great success with many clients and their dogs.

# Lee's Recommended Best Buys

Photo by Cristina Anne Costello

# Snuffle Mat

- Great for foraging, fun and rewarding for all dog breeds

- Thicker lifted strands make it better at hiding kibble treats

- Suction cups for attaching to flooring, to stop sliding about when snuffling

- Machine washable and durable

# GPS Dog Tracker

- Waterproof design which fits on the collar

- Live GPS tracking with unlimited range (monthly subscription)

- Set location safe zones for notifications

- Monitor activity as well as sleep patterns

# Reusable Toilet Training Pads

- Perfect for toilet training and less waste for land-refill

- The design helps minimise odours which helps keep freshness

- Non-slip design for laminate surfaces

- Reuse again and again.  Ingenious

# Slow Feeder Bowl

- Helps slow down your dog eating too quickly, prevent choking, vomiting, overeating and indigestion

- Slip-proof base.  Good design

- Highly resistant and tough design

# NylaBone

- Perfect for teething and stopping mouthing of the hand when used alongside training and Coffee wood, and crinkle plush toy

# Snuggle Puppy

- Perfect for puppies in the crate at night time.

- Works as a comfort aid towards dogs with anxiety

- Gives warmth with a heartbeat, which helps your dog to relax

# Good Selection of Toys

- Reasonable toys for teething and play

- Rope toys are sturdy and last longer than some fabric/plastic toys

- Some of the toys in this pack aid good dental health

- Natural cotton fibre and good materials

# Petkit Water Bottle

- 400ml leak proof handy dog water bottle

- The filter system removes residual chlorine and absorbs impurities

- Easy to clean

- I highly recommend this water bottle.

# KONG

- Perfect for teething puppies

- Can help with anxiety, including Separation

- I HIGHLY recommend this for all dogs

# Doorbells Toilet Training

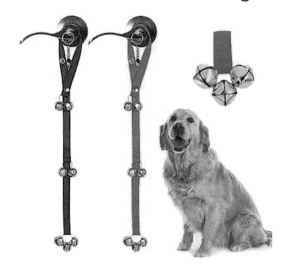

- Perfect for training your dog to let you know when they need to go out.

- Training with the bells is about you engaging, showing and lots of patience. Also once your dog gets it – he/she will also ring it to go out play – assess and understand when your dog actually does go toilet. This will allow you to ignore the times where your dog just wants to play, else that bell will just keep ringing loads.

# Plush Crinkle Fun Toy

- Perfect for teething, should help to stop chewing on fabrics.  I highly suggest combining this with Coffee Wood and a Nylabone.  Avoid sprays as they tend to not work.

- Highly durable

- No stuffing inside

- Easy to clean and you can put them in the wash

# Brain Training Puzzle Toy

- Fun puzzle toy to give mental stimulation and boost your dog's IQ

- Can help towards relieving anxiety and stress

- Easy to assemble, maintain and sturdy

# Wobble Ball with Sound

- My Sparty absolutely loved his. Kept him busy for hours and made me laugh and smile a lot as well. Highly recommend

- Your dog will play with this toy for hours

# Toilet Training Tray

- Perfect for toilet training if you live in an apartment, high-rise, or place where you have to access to back garden

- You can easily train your dog to go on the toilet tray

- Easy to clean.  Urine goes straight into the tray area, everything else remains on the artificial grass

- Can easily move about

# Recordable Training Buttons

- Perfect for training and boosting your dog's IQ

- Helps with dog-to-human communication

- Is fun and engaging.  Highly recommend

# Yak Chew

- Great for your dog – rich in protein and calcium

- Yak's last ages.  Your dog should love it

- Can sometimes help with teething, however for teething best to go with plush crinkle toys, Nylabones and Coffee wood

# Halti Training Lead

- Fantastic for training.  HIGHLY recommend – I use this lead generally for training all ages and breed of dog.

- The quality is good.  I get my clients to purchase this lead all the time.  So many training techniques can be done with the lead.  Highly durable.

- Comes in large and small, black and red

# Flexi Classic Retractable Lead

- Quality of this retractable lead is fantastic. I highly recommend for all dog owners who want a retractable lead.

- Not ideal for lead control training, however I do use Flexi for the Come Away command, as it works perfectly for that technique

- Good value for money

# Whizzclick Clicker for Training

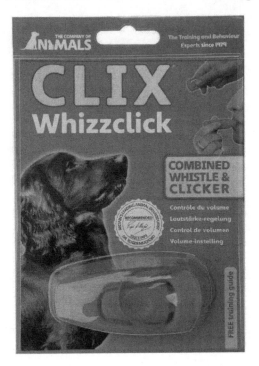

- HIGHLY recommend Whizzclick. I get all my clients to use this, and I also use it when training advanced techniques, combined techniques and dance routines with Spartacus.

- Unlike some of the clickers on the market, I have never needed to replace it. Highly durable and manufactured well.

- Clicker training is a must. Helps further into the future to educate quickly and boost your dog's IQ

When two dogs fight over a bone

A third carries it away

I would like to thank all the people whose photography has been included in this book.

Cover Photo

T.R Photography

Section Photos

Jane Almon, Andrew Pons, Jamie Street, Wade Austin Ellis, Imelda, Mohan Vamsi Somireddi, Victor Grabarczyk, Anna Dudkova, Edson Torres, Elisa Kennemer, Alvan Nee, David Clarke, Sergey Semin, Alison Pang, John Price, Emily Star, Chris Arthur-Collins, Valentin Balan, Ayla Verschueren, Brooke Cagle, Sarandy Westfall, Connor Home, Brina Blum, Tallie Robinson, Fernando Nuso, Justin Veenema, Angel Luciano, Laura Baker, Martin Blanquer, Matthew Fournier, Noah Buscher, Claudie-Ann Tremblay-Cantin, Matthew Hamilton, Gabrielle Costa, Louis-Philippe Poitras, Luke MacGillivray, Lydia Tan, Anna Kumpan, Austin Wilcox, Kyle Mackie, Amber Aquart, Jordan Bigelow, Carissa Weiser, Wannes De Mol, Roberto Nickson, Alexander Grey, Reed Shepherd, Edgar Chaparro, Cristina Anne Costello, Bruce Warrington, Karsten Winegeart

All photographs are from unsplash.com, and are free to use under the Unsplash License

The products recommended by Lee Richards are those that Lee is aware of as having true benefits for many dogs whom Lee has trained or been assisting with. This does not mean that other products aren't to the same good standard. Lee's recommendations are based on experience, knowledge and understanding, so people can reach results that Lee is aware of. In addition, please be aware that products suggested a commission may be given to Lee, but this is not the reason for suggesting. This very small commission just helps towards the cost of writing this and future books. Thank you

Printed in Great Britain
by Amazon

30797510R00121